# UNSTOPPABLE

## Living The Life
## You Are
## Intended to Live

REGINA JOHNSON
MINISTRIES

# Regina A. Johnson

# UNSTOPPABLE
## Living The Life You Are Intended to Live

Regina Johnson Ministries
2015

Unless otherwise indicated, Scripture quotations are taken from the New International Version of the Bible. Holy Bible, New International Version. Copyright 1973, 1978, 1984, 2011 by Biblica, Inc. All rights reserved.

First Printing: 2015

Printed In the United States of America

ISBN 978-0-578-15696-5

Regina Johnson Ministries

Graphics done by LCR

Photography done by Frank Harrison

# Dedication

I would like to dedicate Unstoppable to the women of My Time, whose lives I've watched change and develop over the past year. To The Fathers House for all the love and support, encouragement you have given me in my journey becoming an author. To my many friends who inspire me, pray for me and encourage me daily. To Pastor Lloyd Maddoux, Pastor Elaine Benson, Pastor Lisa Wells, Dr. Josie Carr I want to say Thank You, because I could have never began this journey without the Lord and You in my life.

To my loving husband Joe and to my five wonderful children Markus, Riley, Jordan, Nick and Chaselyn. To my sibling Sheree Salazar and my precious mother Tommie West. You can be found between the lines of my life bearing up love, support and encouragement and I thank you for it and love you even more. I could not have made it this far without you, not to mention all you have added to my life that makes this book possible. To my God kids we did it!

# Contents

# Foreword

If you are ready to move forward and live out your purpose and destiny, this book is a MUST read!

*"Unstoppable"* is a masterpiece of timeless revelation. Its profound purpose is to dispel the lies of the devil about you and to eradicate the twisted perception of inadequacy and inferiority that so many Believers confront on a daily basis.

The author, Pastor Regina Johnson, has shared valuable nuggets to assist you in getting to your place of fulfillment. She speaks candidly about her struggles and experiences in hope that the lessons she learned will encourage you to forget the past, forgive others and walk in the truth of God's Word for your life. She challenges you to push the envelope. Abandon all excuses and fear of failing and trust what God has said about you above what anyone else says or thinks.

Congratulations Pastor Regina! You have revealed an understanding of God's love and care for His people that will cause them to move from a place of brokenness to a place of fulfillment and purpose. I am extremely excited about what will happen in the mind and heart of every person who reads this book. They will truly be *"Unstoppable"*!

Josie Carr, Ed. D.

# Introduction

Unstoppable: (uhn-stop-uh-buhl)
Incapable of being stopped.

When I think of unstoppable, a culmination of moments colliding into each other comes to mind. From moments of complete confusion of who you are and where you're headed.

Lies dispelled and utter truths breaking forth in one's life. We were made to be unstoppable. The picture that the enemy paints of us to others can't be compared to the picture we've painted of ourselves.

Our twisted perception of who we are often determines where our journey will end. But when I see the truth and understand how I was beautifully and wonderfully made, then I become unstoppable.

Many of us are focused on how others see us, but how do you see you? How does the One that made you see you? When the truth of that is brought to the light, it is the beginning of a life that is unstoppable.

The enemy fights us. He throws barriers up before us, great smoke screens before us to prevent us, not just from succeeding, but also from becoming unstoppable.

When does unstoppable happen? The best way that I can describe it is, when you're in a place, living day to day, and an opportunity comes along allowing you escape and experience what God has truly called you to do.

Whether that place was a great success or a complete failure, it cries out for you to come back and try again, because there, you are unstoppable. You just have to learn how to move in it, walk in it, live in it...unstoppable. God created us to be unstoppable.

That's why you see businessmen and women who have great wealth lose it all get up and risk it all again. They show up in that place where they had victory, because for one moment they were able to experience what they were created for.

When you rest in the place where you were created, an awakening happens within you that nothing else will satisfy. That's when you become unstoppable.

# Chapter 1

## Ṝ

# The Glimpse

Unstoppable is in us. I firmly believe that God always gives us a glimpse of where we are headed. Many times we don't recognize it as being the preview, like for an upcoming movie.

Clearly, we sit inside of the theatre specifically for the feature film, but before we are allowed to see what we are there for in that moment, we are shown a glimpse of what's to come.

That preview is to stir us. To make us excited for what's ahead. In Isaiah 46:10 God says "I make known the end from the beginning..." He not only reveals things that will come to pass in a spiritual perspective, but also, things that concern our natural lives.

He takes pleasure in showing us the things He has in store for us and for our own well-being. He reveals it in glimpses, partly because He knows what it truly will take in order for us to stand in the place that He has prepared for us. Quite honestly, if we could see all the things we will have to endure to be deemed equipped we would probably run.

## From the Prison to the Palace

I remember a season in my life when I was basically homeless. One of the most difficult times I've ever had to go through. During that time, I was in a dysfunctional relationship and I was at one of the lowest points in my life. The thing that held me was that I knew I was better than where I was. I knew that because there was a fire that always stayed ignited in me; a vision that stayed before me, not where I was in that moment, but where God had shown me. My glimpse.

One day after being evicted I stood in the middle of the road and wondered what was next. I remember looking to the sky and screaming at the top of my lungs, "I am your kid! You said you would always be there for me. You would never leave me!" And though I felt abandoned in that moment, I knew there was something greater because I had seen it. Many times I had seen it. That gave me the courage and the fight to get up and keep pushing towards what I saw.

Throughout my life there have been people in place to encourage me and tell me what they saw, but the thing that held me was the glimpse of what I had seen. Others encouraging you is definitely needed, but the thing that holds you is what comes from God.

In the Bible there's a young man named Joseph, whose father was Jacob. Joseph found favor in the eyes of his father because he was born to him in his old age. When his brothers recognized that their father loved Joseph more than the others, they despised him.

In Genesis 37 it talks about Joseph having a dream, and when he told his brothers, they hated him the more. *Genesis 37:5-11*

*He said to them listen to this dream I had. We were binding sheaves of grain out in the field when suddenly, my sheaf rose and stood upright while your sheaves gathered around mine and bowed down to it. His brothers said to him, do you intend to reign over us, will you actually rule us, and they hated him all the more because of his dream and what he had said. Then he had another dream and he told his brothers listen he said I had another dream and this time the sun and moon and eleven stars were bowing down to me, when he told his father as well as his brothers his father rebuked him and said what is this dream you had, will your mother and I and brothers actually come and bow down to the ground before you? His brothers were jealous of him, but his father kept the matter in mind.*

In that moment Joseph was receiving his glimpse of where God's plan for his life was headed. The glimpse only showed the end results, it did not show the full journey of where He was taking him. From that point on, Joseph would experience great trials, moments of betrayal and imprisonment, before the vision or glimpse of what God had shown him concerning his future would come to pass.

But in Joseph's heart, despite everything that he had gone through, he did not forget the vision that God had given him. Even though I'm sure many times it looked as if it were only a dream. Maybe even something that he possibly thought of himself, because nothing in his life looked quite like what he had seen.

The Bible clearly shows that from the beginning when Joseph first saw the glimpse and during the journey to the fulfillment of the vision, he had many opportunities to give up on what he had seen, but he never let go of what God had shown him in his heart.

For many of us, God has given glimpses of where it is that He desires to take us, but because the journey is not easy, some choose to abandon it. Great transition has to take place from the glimpse to the glory.

For example, Joseph was shown the dream during a season when he was only tending sheep, but God's plan was to take Joseph to the palace. Can you imagine the transition that had to take place in order to take Joseph from tending sheep to becoming the second most powerful person in Egypt? That's where many of us are today. God is trying to take us from the field to the palace.

As a child, I remember adults asking children what they wanted to be when they grew up. To me it seemed like everyone knew exactly what they wanted to be. With confidence they would answer a teacher, a nurse, a doctor, but I never could say. I didn't see what the other kids saw.

As a matter of fact, I remember talking to my mom and she asked me the same question and I told her all I see are lights. I didn't know what my future held but all I could see were lights. Often times a glimpse is just that. It's not a full picture of every valley and every hilltop. Our glimpse stands as a beacon of light shining in the darkness and leading us in the direction that we should go. For example, God will remind you that you will be the CEO of your own company while you're still sitting in a cubicle at your nine to five. While you are diligently completing tasks and working long nights completing projects to fulfill someone else's dream, but in time what you saw will come to pass. The glimpse stands as a reminder that where I am is temporary. A glimpse is what I hold on to as I patiently wait for my turn.

I may catch glimpses of where I'm going from other people. When I look at them they may serve as a reminder of where God is taking me. It may come through the words being spoken by a great orator or an inspiring writer. Words, people, and even places can be used by God to remind me that there is a place greater than where I am that is beckoning me to come.

For example, when I bought my house I loved it. It wasn't my dream home, but I was grateful for it and blessed to have it. As years passed I became comfortable in that place and soon lost sight of what God had shown me. And then I saw it. The 20-foot ceilings, the master suite over the veranda leading out to a beautiful waterscape pool, and breathtaking view of the lake. I saw a picture and was instantly reminded of where I was supposed to be.

What happens most times is that when we catch our glimpse the fire and passion for what we've seen begins to fade, and it becomes our responsibility to hold on to what was shown to us. Not settling for Ishamel when clearly God has promised Isaac.

I've stood on many platforms in my life. Under many lights. From being a professional dancer, to singing to preaching. It wasn't until I stood under a certain set of lights, in a place where it seemed like I was losing, but in actuality I was winning. That was the moment when I knew that the lights that I had seen as a child, weren't all of those other places, they were merely lights leading to the lights. Moments leading to the moment. All of the other places that I had stood under the lights were not it. The glimpses that God is showing you will meet up with where you are headed. On that day, everything within in you will scream, this is what I saw.

So have you seen it? The glimpses? Has He shown you? Take a second to ask yourself what the Lord is showing you. What is it that when you get close to that place it ignites something within you? Not the place that you've settled upon, because you were too afraid of what you saw at one point in your life but the vision in which God showed you.

Picture this: God enters into a room of where you are and escorts you to a window and through it you can see all that He has in store in for you. Now ask yourself, what did I see? Was it a business? Did you see yourself on TV?  Or performing surgery? Were you inside a stadium? Were you in the cockpit of a 757? Were you performing on Broadway? What was it that you saw? Maybe you were destined to write a New-York Times best seller? Open a school? Become a first-generation graduate? What did He show you?

As a pastor, I've asked several people the question, "What is your dream?" Many of them would answer, I don't have one. I found that so difficult to understand. How can you live without a dream? Now I understand why. Circumstances of life came in and overshadowed the vision of where God desired to take them.

Sometimes its poverty, brokenness from abuse, or just a culmination of disappointment after disappointment that wipes out the memory of what God showed them because God always gives man a glimpse.

# Chapter 2

## Ṝ

# The Help

**Y**ou know how you know that there's something you're supposed to do, but you're just not sure of what it is? I mean you're on the right street, but you don't know which house it is or which door to go through.

I always knew I had a call on my life but I was unclear of what it was, but I was willing to do whatever God had called me to do. If you had asked me what I was going to do in the beginning of ministry I would have said a youth pastor because that's what I was doing at that time.

As a matter of fact, I remember having a conversation with my cousin and her telling me that she knew without a shadow of doubt that God called her to be a pastor. I remember looked that I know convincingly that God has not called me to be a pastor, I'm certain of that. Yet, here I am today.

## Putting the Building Blocks Together

When the Lord began to show me that I was truly called to preach the gospel I knew that I would have to eventually tell my grandfather, who was my pastor at the time. And because of the structure of the ministry in which we were in, what God was showing me, would not be an easy conversation to have, because there were no women ministers at that time.

So after a great deal of contemplation one evening, I went to my grandparents' home and shared with my grandmother and grandfather that I strongly felt that God was calling me to preach. I remember my grandfather laughing and saying, "Maybe he's calling you to be a missionary, I don't think he's calling you to be a preacher." I remember turning to my grandmother wanting her to defend me because I knew that they could see that I had a great passion for Christ. But I also wanted them to see that I was called to preach. And even though her words were gentle and kind she could not confirm nor dispute my calling. At the end of that meeting I remember getting up from the table, walking out of the house and promising myself that I would never mention it again. For the next couple of years I continued doing ministry in the same capacity.

One morning while I was at work, I found myself listening to this preacher on the radio in the same city where I lived. He was powerful. The words and scriptures that he used seemed to leap out of the radio and enter into my heart every time he spoke. Just listening to him stirred me for something greater.

I decided after a few more times of listening to him, that I would visit his church during an 8:00 service so that I would not miss service at my church which started at 11:00. When I entered into that building for the first time, the presence of God was so strong I found myself weeping through the entire service. It was as if God had become tangible to me in that place. The more I visited, the clearer it became to me that I was going to have to make a move, and that was going to be one of the most difficult decisions I would have to make as a young adult. Little did I know God was putting my help in place. The very thing that would help propel me into ministry as a pastor. It was exactly what I needed in that season of my life; it was the place where I would go and stretch and be stretched. The place where I developed my spiritual gifts. Where the voice of God would be made clear to me as I journeyed.

Again, I was going to have to talk to my grandparents. When I went to speak to my grandfather, I was so afraid, but I knew it was something that must be done.

By this time my grandfather could see that I was growing spiritually in ways that could not be addressed at our church. Although he never said it, I believe he was somewhat relieved that I would be somewhere where I could be helped in ways that he could not.

My grandmother, on the other hand, was the tough one. She told me that she thought that I would at least wait until she died to leave the family church. Now that was a hard one. But even with that, I knew it was time.

I became a new member of this church that is still my covering to this day after over 20 years. My life began to be transformed. I began to grow spiritually in leaps and bounds, and my call was becoming clearer to me and others around me. However, I still never openly expressed that God had called me to preach. I was very active in the choir and special events, which opened the door to a few opportunities that stretched my natural talents. One of those doors allowed me the opportunity to tour for five years alongside two other ladies from the church, with an up and coming Christian artist.

After one of our trips, we had to drop the artist who we were touring with off at the airport. My friend Sandra, who was also one of the singers, began to discuss various topics from the Bible, and I remember one of the things we discussed was Revelation.

While she was speaking, it was as if I could see these forces that were holding my mind from being able to grasp a clearer understanding of the word being blown away. By the time that we made it back to her home I was in tears. While she ran into her house to get some things she needed for church that evening I stayed in the car. In those moments I began to cry out to God and tell Him, whatever you want to do with my life, you can do it. Whatever You want from me, I'll give it. In that moment, I heard the voice of the Lord speak loudly within me saying, you've not done what I told you to do seven years ago. This conviction came over me along with fear because I knew when I got to church that evening I needed to tell my pastor that God had called me to preach. Church that evening moved as if it was created just for me. The presence of God moved in a way that was conducive for all hidden giftings, calls and anointings to be birthed forth, drawn out, uncovered, and revealed.

There is a song that says, "If you can use anything Lord, you can use me."
I went to the altar after my pastor made an appeal for those that felt they were being called into ministry to come. Standing there before him with tears lapping down my cheeks, when he laid hands on me and prayed over me, I leaned forward and said pastor, God is calling me to speak. Still too afraid to say preach. After service, the Spirit of the Lord would not let me rest because it was time for me to be forthcoming. I needed to paint the clear picture of what God was calling me to do. All night I tossed and turned knowing that I needed to set up an appointment, sit down and tell my pastor then what I had told my grandfather before. When I arose the next day, I called his office, and asked if there was any way he could talk to me immediately. And of course they said yes, because at this time in our relationship I was no longer just one of the parishioners, I was like one of his

kids, so I went. When I went in his office I asked if we could not meet in there, but if we could talk in the sanctuary and he said sure.

As we entered into the sanctuary I reassured him that I wouldn't take up much of his time but that I needed to be completely honest about what God had spoken to me and what my call really was. Even though I was afraid, I knew the moment was now. God had orchestrated this time before this person for my call to be birthed out.

After I shared with him what God had said, he told me that he knew and began to give me instructions on what would take place next. I wish I could say that from that moment until now, it went quickly, but it didn't.

The help that he would give me in that moment really didn't seem like help at all. As a matter of fact, he told me that he needed me to sit for a year. Now for someone who has been waiting to share what God has been calling you to do for seven years, clearly you wouldn't see that telling you to be seated for a year as help.

As a matter of fact, shortly after he gave me the instructions, the Lord moved my husband and I to a completely different state, and placed me under a completely different minister. I remember kicking and screaming, not understanding why God would have me expose myself and have someone agree to help me, then allow my husband's job to transfer us from Texas to California. I could have said nothing and just waited to get to California.

But it was all a part of God putting the building blocks of my help in place. I couldn't see it then, but I see it now. God putting together all the building blocks of help creating a foundation for me to stand, never allowing me to completely rely on one individual, but learning How to trust Him to be my help and to send me help.

My husband and I were gone only for a few years. And in that place he placed another minister in my life, who immediately saw my call and began to mold me. When my new pastor would ask me to do things that I thought I couldn't do, I would call my former pastor and he would reassure me that what I was being asked to do, the wisdom to do it, was already resting in me.

My time in California was a time of development and growth. It was to help me to become what I needed to be for the next level of my call. The pastor there gave me the opportunity to be stretched in ways that could not have happened at that time where I was. But God knew that place, that pastor, was needed to help develop me. What I have learned is that God will send many people into your life as you journey towards the vision that God has shown you to guarantee your success, our job is to allow the help that has been sent to fulfill its purpose in us, in the season that it's been sent.

When I first went to that church in California my mind was made up to do nothing. I sat on the back row of the church Sunday after Sunday determined not to be seen or heard. Just to receive the word because I didn't want that help. I wanted it to come another way I wanted the one that I had revealed myself to, to help me. Sometimes we miss out on help because we won't be flexible, nor pliable to change. God knows what He is doing and He knows who's needed just for you.

Sometimes it's hard because we don't understand why or we're looking for something different but God know us and the type of help that we need. If I were to pick out the people or places that would help shape my life, that would help me journey to the place that God has shown me, probably most of the people that had been used to help me, would not have been the people or the places I would have selected for myself. Either because of lack of exposure or just the limited wisdom that I had at the time at the beginning of my journey I probably would have chose people who could not have helped me or would have had a desire to. It's almost like, I heard a preacher preach about fasting once when I was much younger, and when he began to preach I became frustrated because I went to a church where fasting was something we did regularly, I felt like sitting there listening to him preach was a waste of my time. But I remember hearing clearly as I was griping about the service, the Spirit of the Lord said, but do you know how to apply it and are you fasting now? Sometimes God puts people in place just to help you to hold onto what you already know, sometimes just to bring new information to you. In other times to help mold, shape, and maybe even just challenge you. Like an olive is squeezed to get the better from it, many times that's what your help does. It brings out the best in you. You don't need help becoming an olive. You need help in bringing what's in you out.

My pastor back in my hometown called me while I was in California and said Regina I have a church for you when you come back. I remember my mind was just blown away. Are you kidding? Like a whole church, a real church? He said yes, when you come back there's a church waiting for you. At that moment, I could clearly see how the pastor in California was being used to prepare me for where I was headed. The funny thing is, my pastor in California thought I was going to be used by him to start a ministry there. Can you see how God works? So, when I moved back to Texas, that's exactly what my former pastor had. A church. It had been given to his ministry. After he tried placing it in the hands of some of my counterparts, he said the Lord showed him that it was for me. When you hear something like that I'm sure the picture in your mind would be that he's going to take you and walk you through, step by step, and if that's not the thought you had, that's the one I had.

I remember him giving me the keys to the building and telling me to go and see it for myself. Can I be honest with you, I was excited about getting the church but being a pastor was not what I saw. I didn't see that coming. I saw myself sitting on the platform with the other ministers, drinking water and eating mints. Only acknowledgement of the call was what I was really after. And once acknowledged I was fine. An occasional speaking engagement was all I was looking for. But God had more. From that day until now, the help that God sent me was not the help that would sit you on its lap and walk you step by step through every challenge it was the help I needed. Whether it came from my senior pastor, my friends, other ministers, the help I needed was a help that made me turn and press in to God. No baby stepping me no pacifier time, it was help like when my father showed me once that I did not know how to swim. He let me jump in to deep waters because as long as I was in shallow waters I was able to deceive myself into believing that I was swimming. But after the water went over my head, I quickly became aware that I needed my father's help and I needed to learn how to swim not just look like it.

The help that God sends may not be what you thought because God will always send you the help you need to fulfill the plan he has for you. It comes in unsuspecting packages daily, but you must be brave enough to unwrap every package that god sends, and open enough to draw from it and properly interpret the purpose of the help that has been sent. Many times we don't think we need help, and often times we reject help because accepting it requires us to embrace the change. Things that need to be corrected, areas where we are weak or dysfunctional are addressed by our help. The sooner we grasp hold of it the moment the teaching the tutelage of our help the quicker we progress to the place where God has called us.

Recognize your help. It may be your coworker, or your mom, your friends in this season, your pastor. There are so many people and things placed before you that are your help but you must recognize it. If you desire to see, walk in stand in the place God has shown you must recognize you cannot get there on your own.

A book, a class, or maybe even an individual holds the piece of the puzzle to where you're headed.

In the Glimpse, I talked about Joseph. Whether he felt like his brothers were helping him or not God was using them to help promote Joseph to the palace, His brothers placed him in a pit which would put him into the hands that would carry him to Egypt. The prison he was placed in helped put him in the position to where his gifts could be recognized. You must see God in all things helping you get to unstoppable.

# Chapter 3

R̄

# Kryptonite

If you've ever seen or read any of the Superman stories, I'm sure you're aware of his extraordinary capabilities. Flying at the speed of light, being able to stop a moving locomotive and leap over buildings in a single bound have all contributed to our belief that Superman was unstoppable. Until he encountered kryptonite.

Superman was originally from the planet Krypton, which was inhabited by an advanced civilization. Over time, the planet self-destructed resulting in Superman's relocation to Earth. From the moment he landed, his natural abilities became even greater causing him to appear to be unstoppable. But isn't it mind blowing that the only thing that made Superman weak or average, were small pieces from his past, otherwise known as kryptonite.

It's amazing to me that it doesn't take something really large, it can be just a small piece of your past that can be deadly to your future. The deadliest things to Superman that took away his power and weakened him, making him average. No longer super, but common, were shard pieces of kryptonite from his home planet Krypton. As I began to research about kryptonite, I found out that there were various types, but all of them were used to make an unstoppable individual stoppable. What is your kryptonite? What is the thing that stops you every time you begin to advance? You don't have to have lived long to encounter your kryptonite. The important thing is identifying it and removing it from your life. Superman was fine as long as he stayed away from kryptonite. But many of us embrace our kryptonite knowing it is deadly to our lives, our dreams hopes and visions.

## The Thing You Can't Shake Off

Kryptonite isn't the loss of a home or car or a job, kryptonite is that thing within in you that every time you begin to journey upwards, out of the place of your struggle, it appears. Its full intent is to weaken you. It causes you to lose your focus. It's not something as simple as the ringing of a phone in the middle of a project, or a neighbor coming over to talk at the wrong moment. It's the thing that you can't shake sometimes for months, years. Countless times I've heard people of all ages say that every time they get started and things are going right, either a certain person from a past relationship, or an old fear or insecurity resurfaces. It's as if you're riding a never-ending rollercoaster.

Like a young woman who was in a relationship with someone who was abusive physically and emotionally and she gets free from him. When she begins to move up in life, and completely moves past it, he shows up. Before she knows it, she's in the struggle all over again. The scary thing about it is, it doesn't happen only once, but multiple times. Every time she begins to rise up from the situation, he shows up again to destroy every opportunity and chance that she may have at reaching success.

Do you know someone who is extremely gifted but never really advanced because the moment the opportunity for advancement comes they are overtaken by fear, self-doubt, or insecurity, and they immediately begin to self-sabotage the moment or opportunity? Thoughts of past failures flood their minds and grip their hearts to the point that they would return to the place where they feel most safe, which in actuality is, mediocrity. Their fear becomes their kryptonite. It doesn't arise until they decide to change, to do things differently to raise the bar. The moment they step out of the place that they are in.

I once heard a story of a man whose superiors at his job would constantly try to give him a promotion. But because he was so afraid that if he were to take the promotion, he wouldn't be able to perform as well as he could in his current position, so he allowed countless opportunities to pass him by. Your kryptonite may be thinking more highly of yourself than you are. The inability to control your temper, or your words, only you know what it is.

In the Bible it tells a story of a very strong man named Sampson who was anointed with matchless strength. In a single battle He was able to kill one thousand men with the jawbone of a donkey and pile the men in heaps. He also performed heroic feats such as killing a lion with his bare hands, and destroying enemy troops single-handedly.

The Lord had commanded Sampson's mother before he was even born to never put a razor to his head. That his hair was never to be cut because his strength would lie in his hair. The moment that his hair was cut, his strength would leave him. In the story it tells of a woman named Delilah who was relentless in finding out where Sampson's strength lies. From the moment he met her, he was on a path of destruction. Shortly after he entered into a relationship with Delilah, the philistine rulers paid her to find out where Sampson's strength lied. Using her power of seduction and deception, Delilah eventually wore Sampson down until he finally divulged that he had been set apart by God and had taking a Nazarite vow at birth and his hair was never to be cut. When Sampson told Delilah that his strength would leave him if a razor were to be used on his head, Delilah plotted with the philistine rulers and one night as Sampson lay with his head on her lap, Delilah had a coconspirator to shave Sampson's head. And in that moment Sampson was made weak and Sampson was captured.

Looking at the story you would immediately say that his hair was his kryptonite. And it was. He knew that his hair was his strength and his weakness. Immediately we'd like to say that Delilah was Sampson's kryptonite, but she wasn't. He was his own. Knowing always where his strength and weakness lied. It was Sampson's responsibility to protect what God had given him. Sampson had two vulnerabilities: his attraction to untrustworthy women and his hair. He was physically strong, but morally weak.

Your kryptonite may not be that God has given you great strength and power, but your kryptonite may lie in your character. I've often heard the phrase your gift will take you to places where your character can't sustain. Maybe your kryptonite is that whenever God positions you your character becomes an issue. Not the big lies, but little ones. The ones that shake others' confidence in you enough to make them question your integrity. Maybe gossiping is your issue. Maybe it's as simple as fault finding or backbiting. They too are kryptonite. So look at your life and honestly assess what is that one thing that's always holding you back. Always causing you to stumble, always making you miss out.

One of the things that I have noticed as a common form of kryptonite in believers is a spirit of jealousy. Unable to rejoice in others' victories because we're so angry and frustrated. In the season in which we are in, our jealousies cause us to say things and respond in a way that becomes dangerous not only to others but ourselves. For example, have you ever been new to a church or a job and everything seemed perfect. If it's your church, you feel so blessed to be there. If it's your job you're so grateful that God gave it you. But then someone comes and begins to share with you all the things that are wrong with your coworkers or fellow parishioners and all of a sudden what was wonderful and a blessing no longer looks the same. You have to learn how to protect yourself. Not only from the kryptonite in your own life, but the kryptonite that others carry. I remember in this church that I attended for a short while, new members would come in and would love the service, pastor and the members but there was always this one person who befriended the new members only to share with them everything that was wrong with the church. In no time at all, people who had great enthusiasm and excitement for what God was doing would either leave the church, or their attitudes towards the church would dramatically change. It was as if the person who did this repeatedly was only in the church to taint the newcomers' perception of what God was doing. Clearly, they themselves were kryptonite. It didn't take a group of people, only one individual turned person after person. It doesn't take a lot of kryptonite. Just a little. One small grain of something toxic being deposited, can turn an illustrious vision into nothing at all.

Again I ask you what is your kryptonite? Do you recognize it? Do you see it creeping into your life robbing you of opportunity after opportunity? Do you embrace it? Out of frustration unable to let it go so you hold on to it? Be aware that until you identify and remove the kryptonite you are bound to be held hostage to it, therefore only permitting yourself to move in brief seasons of victory because of it.

# Chapter 4

## R̄

# Let It Go

As women, one of the areas we struggle in the most is just letting go. In the Bible it says there is a season for everything, and I firmly believe that there is also a season for us to just let things go. Letting go is a behavior that we have to learn. It's not just letting go in a relationship between a man and a woman, but even in the workplace. There are times when God will take us to places where we are blessed for a season; however, He will require us to leave in order to take us somewhere greater. Because we are afraid of moving to a place where we cannot see what's going to come next, many times we choose to stay right where we are, prolonging our time in an area that God no longer desires for us to be. We're afraid to step out and find something better, and our fear causes us to go through what God was trying to help us avoid.

In the book of John it tells a story about a woman who was caught in the act of adultery, and according to the Mosaic Law it commanded that the woman be stoned to death. As her accusers were making their case before Jesus, it says that he bent down and started writing on the ground with his finger. And when they began to question him on what was the right thing to do, Jesus said let anyone who is without sin throw the first stone at her, and leaned back over and began to write on the ground again. At that time those who heard what He said, one by one began to walk away until only Jesus was left standing there with the woman. It says that Jesus straightened up and asked her, Where are your accusers? Hast no one condemned you? And she said, no one sir. Then neither do I, He stated. Jesus declared, go now; leave your life of sin. (1)

## Time To Fly

When we look at this passage, we see a woman who was given the opportunity to let go of a life that would bring her death and change how she would see herself from that point on. Could you imagine being caught in a sin and being brought to an open shame before people? Would you be able to forgive yourself? Furthermore, could you forgive them that brought you there? Some of us are having a difficult time, not only forgiving others, but forgiving ourselves. In order to move forward, for some, it's easier to forgive others than to forgive yourself. Jesus asked the lady, where are your accusers? And her reply was, there aren't any. If we were asked the question, "where are your accusers?" and responded there aren't any, it would not be accurate because one would remain. And that accuser would be our self. Our inability to let go of things that we brought upon ourselves which cause shame, embarrassment, and personal disappointment, is what lingers on in us as we try to move forward.

There was a time in my own life where I had a plan that fell apart. The pain and disappointment that came with it was unbearable. It wasn't the judgment of others that held me bound in a place of disapproval; it was my own thoughts toward myself. Have you ever felt like you let your own self down? You had the ability to succeed in that moment, but you failed yourself? No matter how people tried to encourage me during that season, I couldn't hear because I'd already formed my own opinion concerning myself. Instead of just letting go, I held on and allowed one moment in time to rob me of several years of my life. If I had been the woman who was in the process of being stoned, when everyone else left, I would have been standing there to stone myself. That is what happens so many times. We have been released to go and do greater, but we are our own enemies, our own stumbling block. We're the very ones who hold ourselves back, and remind ourselves of past failures. We embrace that image in the mirror and see failure instead of recognizing the place where we have fallen as a mere moment in time. Rather than getting up and advancing past the hurt and brokenness that was a part of that moment, we refuse. If no one else would point the finger, we would point it at ourselves. It's my own thinking. It's me who needs to let go of me! What a sad scenario; an individual unable to advance and their very captor is their own being. the jailor to the prison in which they are trapped, and they hold the key. When we are dealing with ourselves, it's a hard battle to win. Once we form an opinion that's unhealthy concerning us, regardless of what's spoken to us or over us, we have the ability to reject it and see ourselves in an unfavorable light. It could be something as simple as getting a new hairstyle, sitting on another side of a room, or talking to someone you've never talked to before. Moving doesn't always mean packing up your belongings and relocating to another state. Moving can simply be coming out of a place where you are stuck. A place that will enhance your life in one way or another. It's silly when you think about it. There are women who wore the same hairstyle in high school. Now in their 60s, their hair is still cut the same, curled the same, their eye shadow still looks the same, because they are afraid of change. When I move from the place where I was comfortable, I am required to learn how to operate in a new way. I have to see myself different. I have to put myself in an uncomfortable place to become comfortable at a new level.

We have to be able to see that the moment is ending and change is coming. It's time for something new. Because we have such a difficult time releasing what is behind us, we hinder ourselves from fully grasping what's ahead. You can't take flight and soar into the air while tightly gripping something that is on the ground. Picture this: A bird trying to fly while one of its legs is tied to something on the ground. It will only be able to rise to the height of the length of the chord in which it is tied. I cannot tell you how many times I've been fearful of being able to move forward into something new. How can I ever become unstoppable if I am stuck? Stagnant in a place that no longer brings forth anything good to my life. (Let it go). In order to enter into this place of unstoppability we must maintain our fluidity. Just because that place brought forth great blessings in seasons past, there comes a time to let go. It has to come to an end, very much like Elijah when he hid out at the Kerith Ravine. The Lord sent him there for a season and had ravens take him bread and meat in the morning and the evening and he drank from the brook. A time came when the brook dried up and God instructed him to move on. If he had not moved the resources in which he needed would not have been provided. God did not have him move without preparing resources ahead of him. See when God tells us to let one thing go, you can believe that He has already been working on a greater blessing in your future.

During a counseling session I was facilitating, a young woman who was bound in her emotions, full of anger and bitterness because she was unable to let go, stopped her ability to reach the level of success that God was calling her to. As she tried to move forward in her life- and I must say she was very talented in her craft, very beautiful in appearance-she was not capable because her bitterness had apprehended her. Every place in which she was wounded whether big or small, she held on to every action that was inflicted upon her. When I brought it to her attention that the real problem was her inability to forgive, she couldn't see it. She did not recognize that she was holding people hostage and severing relationships. She needed to progress, but felt justified in her actions towards the individuals that wounded her to the point that she had placed herself in a box and didn't even realize it. The number of people that she refused to forgive was growing. Can you imagine trying to move forward in your career, or even in your personal life, and not being able to forgive anyone who hurt you? It seems ridiculous to a healthy mind, but I have seen people walk away from wonderful opportunities due to their refusal to forgive and let go of the people who hurt them. It's like winning a paid vacation, but refusing to take it because someone you couldn't forgive was going to be at your destination. The only person that's suffering is you. Just let go!

The price is too high to pay when we choose not to let go. I have learned in my own life that for the betterment of myself and others, it's best to let go. Let go of the hurt, let go of the fears. There comes a time when we all have to make a decision to let go or remain captive to old places. God required Abraham to let go of his father's religion, the comfort of being with his family and move out into unfamiliar territory, letting go of everything in order to see what God had promised him. It may be scary at first, but God would not require you to let go if He didn't have something greater in store. So again I say, **just let go**.

The word of God says that He would never leave us nor forsake us, so if He's telling me that greater is on the other side of where I am, I have to know that it doesn't mean I'm alone. Letting go doesn't mean letting go of His hand but wherever He is sending me, He will be there. What is it that you are afraid of letting go of? Better yet, what is it that He has told you that you need to let go of in order to progress? Haven't you wasted enough time allowing your emotions to hold you in a place that God is beckoning you to come out from? Begin to say to yourself, I too will come out from among them. My fears of failure, my fears of being alone, my fears of rejection; I will come out from among those places and see all that God has promised me.

Like a tightrope walker, I will let go of things and start my journey, one step in front of the other. I will release the place that's safe, the place that's comfortable, and begin to move gracefully along, knowing that God has me and that I will not fall. I'll move from one destination to the next, knowing that I will arrive at the very place God has planned for me. It is so sad to encounter individuals who are afraid to let go of their past, to see them struggle to hold on to places and people that are no longer beneficial to their lives. Countless faces with tears streaming down their cheeks, and the simple heart of each of their issues is their inability to release, and grasp hold of the new. If only they could see how wonderful it is beyond this place of where they are stuck. I grew up in a small town, but within a 200mi radius of that city are two of the largest cities in the US. One of them is only about 35 miles from my township.

To this very day there are people who live in my town, that have never traveled there simply because they were afraid of the unknown. Afraid of the freeway, afraid of getting lost once they entered into the city, and afraid of what they may encounter because of what they heard. They remain stuck in the small box that is our town. The funny thing is, as time progresses, that city is growing at such a great rate that it is causing the other counties around it to expand and that is very exciting to those who are able to move in and around the city. But those who remain in my township are completely unaware of the great transition taking place around them simply because they are afraid to travel beyond where they live. I'm sure God didn't intend for us to live this way. There are so many things that are beyond where are that God wants us to experience, but many of us won't because we can't let go. God tells us that we can do all things through Christ. When we feel ourselves being stuck in places, we say I don't know what to do. It's as simple as moving forward, releasing yourself or just letting go. When I speak with people concerning letting go, the reason they don't want to is maybe they ended up there trying to prove to others that what they were doing was right, and then the outcome is something bad. Because they are so afraid of how they would look in the eyes of others, they remain in that place.

In my first marriage, I was truly a victim of that. My family and my friends tried to talk me out of getting married, it really didn't have anything to do with him, it was the reason I had chosen to get married at that time. The real motive behind my decision was because my father died, and I was looking for someone to replace him.

Everyone could see what I was doing except me. So when the bottom fell out of my marriage I was too ashamed to say that they were right, so I remain wed in a relationship just to prove to others that I had not made a mistake. In hindsight, it was one of the craziest things I could have done. Not only was I being held captive, so was he. Is that your story? Are you stuck somewhere just trying to show others that your previous decisions were not the wrong ones? Is your pride in the way? Are you afraid of what they will say or think concerning you? God gives each and every one of us a door of escape. Whenever we reach a place He doesn't want us to be it is our responsibility to see it, recognize what it is and exit.

Your life will be filled with many opportunities but when a season ends just let it go.

# Chapter 5

Ṝ

# My Moment

In my teens and much of my young adult life I was one of those people that you hear about that was often trying to find themselves. You know the people that graduate from high-school and college, and have to go off and find themselves? That was me. I was always trying to find that thing in me. So like most people I tried different careers, moved to different cities, looking for that thing you're supposed to find when you're finding yourself. Saying that I get a visual of that young male that has the backpack on his back and he's taking off for this new adventure, backpacking from state to state in hopes to experience this moment of awakening, trying to answer the question of who he is.

What I've come to find out is that there is a moment that waits for each and every one of us where we can say in the midst of that awakening that I was made for this. For some it comes early on and others much later in life. But if you don't give up searching for it, it will come. I remember my moment when the clarity of who I was and what I was made to do came in to focus. It happened while I was in the midst of just being obedient to God and journeying in life with an open mind that God would lead me to wherever it is that He created for me. I began to journey towards that moment while I was living in California. I remember the Lord telling me that while I was there my job was to do my part in helping my husband find success in his career. Now when I say that, it means that God wanted me to do things that I didn't even know how to do. If I began to describe what it is, you would shake your heads and say surely I was joking. I'm probably the least girly girl, domesticated female that you would find. I'm not a great cook, not a great housekeeper, so when he asked me to iron-not send his uniform to the cleaners-but iron he knew it was going to require something out of me that I did not know how to do, but I was willing. I could see in my husband's eyes that he wanted to advance in his career and through conversations that we had had I knew he was ready to obtain what he had been praying for because clearly God was listening so the Lord was showing me my part in helping make that happen. All the while God was also preparing me for my moment. The thing that God was calling me to actually has nothing to do with ironing or cooking or even cleaning as far as that matters, but in order for Him to show me what He had for me, I had to allow Him to position me in such a way so my husband's dreams would be equally as important.

It's amazing that when God gets ready to place your moment in your hands to get you ready for what He is preparing you to do, He will position you to help someone else's dreams come forth.

## The Place You Searched for All Your Life

I'm reminded of the day I was sitting in my living room looking out of my bay window at the mountains when the Lord began to speak to me concerning a work He wanted me to do. Immediately I became excited at the opportunity because I could feel this churning on the inside of me. A sense of knowing that I was on my way. Everyday God would begin to show me more and more about what it was that He wanted me to do. He would give me instruction for what I needed to take care of as I made preparation for the event. There would be days where I would just be in awe at the fact that God would call me to do an event at the magnitude in which He was, and then others I would be scared out of my mind thinking to myself I am clueless on how to get the project done even with God's help. During that time I was still trying to figure out my real place in life, what I was truly called to be so I was fearful of making a mistake saying it was God and then it turned out not to be. He didn't move fast with me the process of this took actually two years I felt like someone that was pregnant carrying a baby beyond term, looking forward to the moment for when it would come, sharing with others what God had shared with me. Still all the while, working towards what was to come. This event in which God had given me would involve me trusting God and being led by God at a level that I never had before. And the one thing that is so dangerous when you are trying to find yourself in the midst of God trying to show you who you are, you have a tendency to lean and depend upon the opinion and views of others. Because you are in a new place you're always looking for someone to validate you.

It is important that when God is speaking to you concerning you that you lean in to God and less into man because though they would desire to tell you the paths to take to get to where God is taking you if they have never journeyed there before, they really cannot properly instruct you. What I have learned is that good people that love you desire to protect you, and try to advise you as best as they can but if they have never been to where you are headed they cannot instruct you properly; Thus setting you up to fail. It's amazing that when God is instructing you how many opportunities arise for you to follow other paths than the one God is calling you to. What I've learned is the other paths may even look right or better, maybe even safer, but if it is not God's designated path it will not take you to your moment in time of what God is doing with you and who you are. Many times we mistake doing what God said to do by doing what He said for us to do in our own way. God was taking me to an "aha" moment like one of those moments when you've been walking around in a dark home with the lights cut off groping for the switch and then your hand lands upon it. All of a sudden, you can see when you couldn't see before. A place of familiarity and in actuality what that is, is a moment when everything within you is telling you I was made for this; this place this time. Even though you've never been there because now you can see and you are able to maneuver easily. It's as if it happens second nature. You move so easily as if you weren't even thinking, it's as if you've been preprogrammed to move in this place, to operate at this level. God was taking me in the direction of my made-for-this moment. I remember when it came close to the unveiling of the work in which God and I had been working on in secret. An overwhelming sense of fear of failing God came over me, and I remember asking God that if I was going to blow it in any way, for us to just not do it. And I remember Him giving me a gentle nudge to keep moving and not to put my trust in man alone, but to keep my trust in Him.

You see, if you journey in this life long enough, to places of successes and failures, you will come to a place of where they are almost even. So even though I had walked with God long enough to know that He would not fail me I had also fallen enough to know that there's a possibility that I could fail Him. Now I know that when you hear that immediately, those of us that are Christians would chime in by saying I would never fail God because he knows what I'm going to do before I do it, so I want to say that's not what I am talking about. I'm talking about him giving me clear direction and still knowing within myself that there was a possibility that I could veer away from the complete instructions in which He had given thus making what I would do not what He had asked at all. Be careful to do exactly what God tells you to do when He tells you and how He tells you. It's very important if you want to show up at the place of where you were created to be and recognize it within a reasonable amount of time. It's easy to get caught up in trying to follow God and failing, than to simply follow God and succeed. When you do that, your life looks like this one big vicious cycle, like traveling on a freeway and continuing to miss the exit in which you were supposed to exit then coming back and continuing to try over and over again. What a waste of time. What a waste of life. The day before the event I was busy taking care of everything for the following day and watching others who were a part of my team preparing for what they needed to have in place for the event to be successful. Inside me there was this great excitement but awareness that what I had waited for was finally here. No backing up, not turning around, it was time to get it done. As the day ended, and people dispersed because all that was left to do really had already been done minus the few workers that were waiting for others to clear out so that they could do their part I took the liberty to just walk around and observe all that had been accomplished up to that point. And I was amazed at how far God had brought me and awestruck that He would use me to do it.

Then all of a sudden, this intense feeling came over me. You know, like the first time when you realize God is talking to you and you hear His voice. It was like that, almost surreal. In that moment, no matter how afraid I was or how unsure I had been, I knew standing in that place I was made for that it was the place I had looked for all my life up to that point. That place that would answer the thing in me that nothing else could fulfill. That place that God had created just for me. The place that with the right tutelage I would see great success. When I look back over that moment now, as I enter into another season that looks very much like that place that time I realize that if I had not experienced that event which by chance to me seemed as if it were a total failure, I would not know what it was that I was running towards.

Because I had experienced it once, I know what if feels like to move and operate as I was designed. And now nothing can turn me from it. I know what I am made for and no one can convince me differently. And when you know you won't settle for substitute places, you always strive for that moment of completeness no matter how far you may drift from it. You may fight tooth and nail to get back to that place of peace in the midst of chaos, of joy, and fulfillment no matter how chaotic.

Sidebar: it's funny that when you are in your place that you were created many times it will look like a complete mess to others, a three ring circus to many, but it will be the most peaceful place for you. Your time is coming. Don't settle. Don't waste your time in places that make you comfortable. Push the envelope. Because God has made you, uniquely designed you for a place in this life that fulfills you like nothing else can. And once you are there, you will find success and no one will ever be able to drive you out. Your "aha" moment. Your moment of standing in the midst of the process of wherever it is when the feeling and thoughts come flooding in that makes you scream to the top of your lungs, I WAS MADE FOR THIS! Your moment.

# Chapter 6

R̄
.

# The Plant

**M**any are stuck or arrested not because of a lifetime of hurt and brokenness in which we can't let go of, but because of one moment in time. A moment in time I'd like to call the plant. One word spoken over us, one unkind deed that was done to us has held us captive for years.

That moment in time I feel was a calculated move of the enemy. A seed that was sown to keep me from reaching my full potential. If you just take a moment to think about it, you'll be able to identify those places where seeds have been planted in you that have taken root. It's the thoughts concerning you that you cannot shake.

That drives your emotions not in a positive way, but in a way that slows down your progress. That hinders you from becoming all that you intended to be.

The enemy is so crafty. Always recognizing the handy work of God. And because he knows Him better than we do, he is always trying to counter the work in which God is doing. His job is to keep us from recognizing how awesome we really are. And how marvelous the work is that God has done in creating us. It's like a beautiful woman who is breathtakingly gorgeous, flawless. But when she was a child was made fun of because of the style of her hair, the way she walked, the timbre of her voice. The enemy sows a seed and every time she looks in the mirror instead of seeing her beauty, she sees the person that was made fun of that day. If the joke was about her hair she's never satisfied with it, if it was about her lips or her nose, that's what sticks out when she sees herself. Instead of seeing how beautifully constructed her face is, like a masterpiece that was created by a skilled artist. She sees flaw after flaw. It's as if the enemy sits and waits for the moment he can infiltrate a thought, a feeling that contradicts the truth concerning us. A parent enraged many times will speak out of their emotions and the enemy will take one word that is spoken, and lower it into the very depths of the child and no matter what the parent says afterwards all of the thousands of compliments that will be poured out, that one seed overshadows all of the good. One conversation between friends easily misconstrued by the hand of the enemy, causing one to feel less than the other, the enemy waits for the opportunity.

## False Belief

I remember when I was a young girl, my mother was standing looking in the mirror, preparing to go somewhere and I decided in that moment to ask her what did she think of me? How did she see me in the context of the way that I looked? Neither of us knew in that moment that we were both being set up. She was being set up so that her words would be misconstrued to where I would not be able to comprehend what she was saying or doing in that moment. I was being set up because the false belief that my mother thought I was unattractive was being sown into the both of simultaneously.

The conversation started off like this:

Mom, do you think I'm beautiful?
Looking at me with a smile on her face she replied, No I wouldn't call you beautiful.
So I continued and asked: Mom, do you see me as pretty? Because surely if she didn't think I was beautiful she would think I was pretty.
Her next reply, no I don't see you as pretty.
In my mind if she didn't see me as beautiful or pretty she must certainly have thought I was cute.
So I asked: Mom, then am I cute?
And she said to me, no I don't see you as cute. When she said that I was devastated because if she did see me as any of these things, I must be ugly.
But she replied, what I see you as is what I would call attractive.
At that age, I felt she said it because she truly thought I was ugly when in fact her true thoughts were that I was beautiful. But because she didn't want me to grow up being vain, she tried not to put a tag on what she really thought of me. But that's not what I heard and clearly not what I interpreted that as. Since I believed that my mother thought I was ugly, I spent the rest of my time

working on my body to ensure that it was at least beautiful. I went through life almost obsessing over the way I was built. I felt there was nothing I could do about the appearance of my face, but I knew that if I worked hard enough, I could guarantee what my body looked like.

I would measure myself almost daily making sure that my measurements were perfect. I would often look at myself in the mirror from the neck down, with and without clothing to ensure that I remained as close to perfect as I possibly could. I would get magazines and cut out pictures of women who I considered to have perfect bodies. And I would strive to look like them. Starving myself at times, over working out at times trying to compensate and have a great body because I believed that I was so ugly. The enemy took one moment in time that my mother was trying to make sure that her daughter whom she believed was beautiful would not grow up to be arrogant and conceited, and twisted her words, breaking my heart and painting an image within me of myself that was far from the truth.

I've heard that beauty is in the eye of the beholder, therefore I may not have been beautiful to everyone else, but I wasn't the ugliest person in the world. But that was how I viewed myself. That lie perpetuated itself in me all the way until I was in my late 40s. When my mother heard me jokingly telling that story, she began to explain to me why she said that, and in that moment the lie of the enemy was revealed. It was a happy moment yet sad as well. Because I would look back at pictures of a beautiful woman, knowing that the face that was smiling on the photograph was thinking about how ugly she was. After my mother shared that with me I remember going home taking one of those pictures and crying. All of those years, I apologized for the days I held my head down as I entered into rooms because I didn't want people to recognize how ugly I was. For the opportunities that I gave away because I thought I was too ugly to stand before people. I remember once getting an opportunity for a modeling campaign with a well-known company, but instead of taking it, recommended it to one of my friends who I thought was prettier than me for the job even though I had been locked in for it. I didn't believe. Regardless of them saying that I was attractive enough to have my face on a product that would be sold nationwide. Inside of me I was afraid someone would look at the photos and say why would they use this girl? I feared that they would remove me because I wasn't able to represent their brand well. I remember my agent being furious with me and could not understand why I would sabotage an opportunity like that.

One moment in time arrested me. Held me bound. Because of one conversation I walked around for most of my life with my hand in front of my face, with my eyes constantly on the ground because I was afraid of what people might say about how I looked. I didn't want to hear that I was ugly or unattractive. Or for someone to tell me that I was beautiful just to boost my self esteem. The enemy had planted a seed that went deep within me that would affect me on many levels. Not just concerning how I looked, but how others would respond to me. When I became older and began to have children, of course having the ability to maintain a perfect body went away.

So just imagine if that's how you validated your worth. The feelings in which I had concerning me, increased. In my eyes there was nothing about me that would make me attractive to anyone. My husband would tell me all the time how beautiful he thought I was, but those words would go in one ear and out of the other.

How could that be true when the very one who gave birth to me didn't see me as beautiful. So every compliment that was made had to be a lie. Because if anyone could see my beauty, it would have been my mother.

When I finally saw the look on my mother's face when I told her what I thought she meant so many years ago, I could see the hurt in her eyes almost as if she was asking me, how could I believe such a thing as if it was almost unimaginable for a mother to not be able to see the beauty in her child. But there I was in that place for many years, because the enemy planted a seed.

There are both young and old who have found themselves stuck in this place that is so contradictory of who they really are because of one word that was spoken into or over their lives. I mean just flat out lies from the enemy.

## A Plant to Hold You in Place

I was listening to a young girl recently, who had a child out of wedlock; explain to me how she had to make a relationship work with a guy she was with because no one else would want her. Those words had been spoken to her by someone who was close to her shortly after she had given birth to her and when the father of the baby abandoned the two of them, those words rang loudest within her. When in actuality men marry women with children every day, but because the enemy planted a seed in her that would give hope to hopelessness and poor self worth she was willing to settle for whoever would come her way. Anyone was better than no one. Because in her mind no one would want her.

Having a child out of wedlock is not the worst thing that could happen to you. But because of the stigmas that have been set in place surrounding it, many believe it is. Their view of themselves is tied to the opinions of others because if you find your validation in the opinions of others, you will always find yourself lacking. Your worth does not come through the opinions of man, but what God says. The enemy desires to pull us away with lies. Planting seeds that will eventually sprout up, birthing forth fear and insecurity. And brokenness beyond repair. Therefore seeing themselves as less than.

Another lie of the enemy, a plant to hold them in place, to stop their movement, their development. Don't get me wrong I believe that God intended for us to marry and then have children but because of poor choices and circumstances of life, babies are born outside of the spiritual order of things. But God's grace is sufficient and it covers all. The enemy does not desire for us to see the mercies of God in the midst of our poor decisions and devastating circumstances that reach far beyond the boundaries of having a child out of wedlock merely just to hold us from becoming all that God intended.

A young woman shared with me that she felt obligated to remain in a relationship with the father of the child even though he didn't truly want to be with her, nor she with him, because by remaining it made her circumstances not look so bad. At least from the outward appearance her family appeared normal in the eyes of onlookers, which is also another deceptive seed which is planted by the enemy. This is to cause us to paint the picture that everything is all right while living a life that contradicts the truth of where we truly are. What would make you set something in motion in your life that would hold you to a place of misery if it were not a plan of the enemy to interrupt all of the many blessings that God has waiting for you?

## Happy Seed

I remember the Lord sharing with me about this thing called the happy seed syndrome. Happy seed syndrome is when someone grows content in believing that if they had the right opportunity they could have become great. The catch is, the reason why they are not great is because they never tested their theory. It's easy to sit back and talk about what we would have or could have done. But if we're too afraid to utilize our gifts at the level that it will require for us to become more than where we are, we will never see it. You see the happy seed syndrome every day in every occupation. It's always that individual that talks about how smart or how gifted they are many believing within themselves that they are smarter or more gifted than those that are around them, but because of their own self doubt or fears they become content with just knowing that they have the ability to do greater, but have become comfortable in that alone. That is exactly where the enemy desires to hold them. You will never see all that God has as long as you are too afraid to find out what it is that he has really placed in you. You have to come to a place to where just telling the stories or dreaming about how great your life could be is not enough. When we realize that by challenging ourselves and breaking through to the place God desires for us to truly be, it not only for us, but for those who are attached to us. I tell the parents in my church to strive to be your kids' hero. Your kids' example of success. Which will require us doing away with the happy seed and grabbing hold of our full potential?

There's a risk that you must take and it comes with finding out that maybe you're not the smartest or the prettiest or the most gifted. So for some it's better if they never find out. They are happy with just obtaining the seed of potential, rather than planting it into the ground to see what becomes of it. The most important thing is not to become the single best. But what if you find out you're one of the best among many? If you never try, you'll never know and that's where the enemy wants to hold us. He plants the seed and makes us think we are not the smartest, prettiest or most gifted so we don't try rather than us challenging who we really are.

The truth is, God has placed something within us that is great and powerful. I remember hearing Bishop TD Jakes preach about being great at your own level. Because when the enemy tries to plant the seed to make me look across the street at someone else's success, I won't feel bad because my goal is to obtain success at my level. Not yours. The seeds that the enemy sows make me run after your dreams at your level, when God intended for me to be the best at the level he created me. In the same sermon, Jakes made the statement that maybe you are a one-gift person. Similar to the parable of the rich man who left all of his talents with his servants. He left one with one, another with two, and another with five. Jakes placed emphasis on being grateful for what you have been given and using that to its fullest potential. The seed that the enemy has sown into our lives is that what we have is not good enough or not valuable. So we treat it as such. But God knew what He was doing when he gave us our gifts. And that it is sufficient to get the job done. As long as I am judging myself based on your gifts and abilities I will see myself as less and the enemy then will have won. Our job is to extract the seed that has been sown into our lives illegally by the enemy. It doesn't matter when it was done. Whether you were a small child or it happened later in life.

God has given you the ability, the power, and the strength to remove every conflicting thought that opposes the truth concerning who you are and what God has for you.  Allow God to sow into you a new seed of His word. In the place of the lie that was sown by the enemy. It's time to for you to become unstoppable.

# Chapter 7

## Ṛ

# Hidden

I believe that this chapter will bring clarity to where many of us are today. Many people feel as if their dreams and visions go unnoticed by God even though He is the one that planted it in our hearts. When there is a lack of movement where we would expect to see things shifting and moving in our lives, we feel that we are being overlooked while we watch others advance around us. We're still praying and still believing, but seeing very little. It's like taking two steps forward and three back, and you can't figure out what it is that's going on in your life that's causing these types of results. So you begin to question yourself. Have I done something wrong? Did I not hear from God? But the truth of the matter is that you did hear from God and you are on course, but God is putting your destiny securely in place so that nothing or no one can disrupt what He has in store for you. Timing is key. It is very important that when God opens the door for you to step into your destiny, where all of the things that are before you can destroy it or throw your destiny off course.

God will make sure you are fully equipped with all that is needed, so you will not forfeit the opportunity by being unable to maintain what He has placed in your hands. I believe that God prepares routes that are unseen by the natural eye. He gently directs us down paths that appear in the natural as though we are going in circles or nowhere at all. When in actuality, we are right where we need to be.

## Being Hidden by God is a Blessing

To be hidden by God is a blessed thing. It's evident that He is covering us and protecting what He has invested in us but to be hidden is a difficult place to reside in because there is this thing on the inside of us jumping up and down saying, "Can't you see me?" Not to God, but to the world. I'm just as good! What I'm doing is as equally as important as what they are doing. What I'm learning in my own walk is to be solely in tune with what God is doing and how God sees me. Staying in rhythm with God's timing so that I do not move prematurely or try to cause myself to advance before He has opened the doors. I'm learning to trust that He has my best interest at hand believing that what He has planted in me will one day come to the surface, where all can see. We must learn how to rest while we are hidden. I don't mean resting in not staying busy, but resting in the arms of God; knowing confidently that everything is alright as long as I stay hidden in God.

In our journey to the place where God is taking us, there will be seasons when He will keep us hidden under His cloak of protection. And often times we don't even realize that that is what He is doing. The Lord has proven to me that in order for us to complete our journeys successfully He has to hide us from others, and sometimes even from ourselves. Hiding us from ourselves keeps us from getting ahead of the plan that God has for us. It's like trying to connect the dots before having all of the information, or making something happen before its time. God will only reveal to us a portion of what He is doing for our own good. Then there are times when He will hide us from others. Often times when we reveal what we are trying to do, or where we are trying to go, if the individual with whom we are sharing this with cannot see you in the place. They will try to discourage you from moving forward because they lack vision for your dream.

There are also times when individuals will become jealous and will misinform you because they don't want you to accomplish your goal. So God will hide you, in order for what He has put in you to be able to come forth in its proper season. Even when you try to expose yourself God will position you in such a way, that they will be unable to see you or identify who you really are. I remember one Sunday, I was allowing one of the associate pastors to preach, and while they were ministering, the Spirit of the Lord was very heavy, and a gentleman who wasn't a part of our flock, entered into the room.

In times past, this man had been very critical of our ministry, and worked very hard to discourage the people from grabbing hold of the vision that had been spoken. When people would listen to him, it would cause the momentum of the ministry to slow down, and the members would lose their enthusiasm concerning the works that God was doing and was going to do. Once he had discouraged the people, he stopped coming around. It took a while for the church to become excited again about God's plan. This time when he entered into the room, he had a very skeptical eye, and it was evident to me that God had a different plan this time. What he was able to do in the past, God was not going to allow it to happen in that season. When the man took a seat and became comfortable as the associate preacher was preaching it was as if the Spirit of the Lord had lifted, and with a natural eye, it appeared that the gentleman's presence had sucked all of the energy and life out of the service. I could tell that the minister was becoming frustrated as he preached. I'm sure he could feel how the service had shifted from excitement to suffocation. The gentleman who had come in began to look around the room as though he was questioning what was going on. Almost as though he knew something was up, but he wasn't sure of what was happening. I remember watching the faces of the people and looking towards the ceiling, and even asking God what was going on. But no answer. After about 15 minutes had passed, the gentleman got up and exited the building. Immediately after the door closed behind him, you could physically feel the presence of the Lord moving through the room and the joy and excitement reentered into the people, just as it was before he came. When I asked the Lord what happened, He shared with me that what happened in the past, wasn't going to happen again. And that what was taking place was that we were being hidden. The Lord began to tell me that He was hiding the works that He was doing for the people so that in the man's eyes it would appear that nothing good was happening, therefore he would not be permitted to stop what was truly taking place like he had done before. The Lord said He would keep us hidden until we were strong enough to stand and nothing or no one would be able to come and stop the works or discourage the people. He referenced that we would be powerful like a locomotive moving rapidly down the tracks and when they saw us coming, we would be moving with such force that it would be impossible to stop us. In that scenario alone, God showed me that in seasons when it seems like nothing is going on in the eyes of others, that we're making no headway, He is merely just keeping us hidden, so that no harm can come to us before we're strong enough to be revealed.

### Can You See Me?

Have you ever been in that place where you're asking why you are being overlooked for the raise you've been seeking? Why are your gifts being

overlooked when you know they are just as great as everyone else's? Or why you feel invisible when you are at gatherings with your peers? Often times it's not that you are inferior to those that are around you; it's that God is simply not ready to reveal you because the work He is doing in you isn't complete. If He pushes you forward too soon the work that He has begun will not be able to be completed, and if He is not permitted to finish the work in us, failure is a certainty. Many times we come to a place where we are a big fish in a small pond. In our minds we feel as if we have arrived, and God permits us to stay there because in that place it builds our confidence, we are strengthened; our mistakes in that place create minimal damage to others and ourselves. It is when others remove me from the place where I am being developed too soon, and exposed prematurely in a place that I have not yet been made ready, when I end up wounding myself and others. Man will move you forward or promote you before your time to benefit themselves, without the full understanding of the impact and with no real concern for your success. In the eyes of man, men are replaceable. Therefore, your duration in the place where you have been promoted is not a real concern of theirs. God's desire is to elevate you and give you success that it may bring glory to Him and present you with a level of influence that will change your life and impact the lives of others for the better. I can
remember in my own life, where it seemed that God was keeping me on the back burner while others were moving forward rapidly and I was asking the question

that many of you are asking today, why isn't He giving me the opportunity that He is giving everyone else? My understanding was that God was no respecter of persons and that what He would do for one He would do for another. Quite honestly I still believe that, but I understand now that not all of us are ready to go through the door of opportunity at the same time, because our calls are different. I've realized that what you are ready for, may take me a little longer. God will allow others to bypass me so that no harm will come to me while He is preparing to present me. There have been times when people have presented me and I was unable to stand. Even though I had the wisdom and ability to do the job, there were others things that God was working on. This prevented me from being able to be at my best in the position that was given to me. I struggled with fear, and I was very insecure, so I sabotaged the opportunity.

See when God hides you, it's so that others won't see you while you're struggling to be made whole. God wants to present a finished product, because that finished product represents His work. Instead of just placing opportunities in our hands merely because we feel that we're ready, God will protect us so that His work won't be destroyed. The Bible references that if you place someone in position before they are ready, it will cause them to become arrogant and fall. That's an example of an individual whom God's desire was to elevate them, but not until He had worked out all that was in the individual that would cause them not to be seen in a positive way. When there is a great call on your life, as we have seen many times in the word of God, the Lord will hide you until your appointed time, so nothing can stop your destiny. He hid Moses, until he was ready to lead the people out of bondage. He hid David, until he was strong enough to become king, even though he was anointed to be king at a very young age. He hid Esther, until He was ready for her to become queen. He hid Joseph, until he became second in command over Egypt. And he hid Christ, until God was ready to reveal him as the Messiah. There is purpose in you being hidden from the world. The enemy would have you to believe that God has forgotten about you and that He has created you and placed you on a shelf. But you're not. Hidden doesn't mean you are forgotten. You're actually being kept for just the right time.

## Great Value

My mother has these glasses that her sister brought her from Hong Kong, and we rarely get to use them. They are only brought out during special times. It's not because she doesn't value them but it's the opposite. She had placed great value on them and they are only used during special occasions. The Lord is not going to just allow your gift to be used up by individuals who don't value what He has placed in you so God will keep you for the right moment. Why don't we take a look at relationships? Don't you think it's funny that you have seen individuals passed over as if no one in the world was created for them, but when God brings the right individual in the right time to them, an unveiling takes place. It was God's purpose for no one else to see them. What many see as rejection, God has put something in place to protect them from the wrong individual coming into their life until their true mate was presented. I have seen both men and women searching and searching, ending up in one broken relationship after another because they kept unveiling themselves to people who could not see them.

To be hidden is God's way of protecting us, reassuring us that the enemy will not rob us of what God has in store for us. So don't be discouraged if it seems like no one can see you or hear you in this season. If it feels like you are groping around in the dark, know that God is hiding His plans, even from you at that very moment. I am so grateful for the many prayers that I have prayed that God did not answer in the season that I was asking for Him to. In His infinite wisdom, He knew I was not ready, even though others were telling me I was. God knew that if I had been positioned in the places I was asking, I would have fallen. I've learned to have peace in God's timing.

When God is ready to unveil you, people who didn't know your name suddenly become aware that you are in the room. Opportunities that have bypassed you multiple times, now come in such a way that you couldn't escape them if you tried. It's as if your name has been released in the wind, being carried from place to place and everyone has now become aware of you and your gifts. So don't be frustrated, everyone has a season of unveiling, but you must go through the season in which you have been hidden to reach it. I've heard ministers say that favor is not fair. What appears in our lives that seems like favor to others is merely an unveiling by God. But what we often see has nothing to do with favor it has to do with God moments that have always been there. But, since we cannot see them due to circumstances that have been in our life that did not permit. It looks as though we've been overlooked. When the doors are opened it looks like favor, when in actuality we were on course headed towards the open door that has been open all along.

At our unveiling, everyone around us, including ourselves, come in to what I like to call an "aha moment." We finally see what all the struggle was about, what all the waiting was about, what all of the delays were about. Causing all to stand and say there was a meaning to this season in which we were hidden, and provoking a praise of gratitude to God whose thoughts are clearly higher than our thoughts.

So be patient and confident in knowing that your unveiling will soon/someday come to pass. Cause truly we were all created to be unstoppable.

# Chapter 8

# Ṝ

# Just Jump

This chapter by far is one of my favorite ones to write, because it's mostly about my youngest daughter, whom if you ever get to meet her, you'll absolutely love. I don't think this child has ever met a stranger. From the time she was born, she had this special thing about her that causes her to press past the norms of life. What I mean is she began talking at an age that she shouldn't have been. Her comprehension was much higher than other children her age. As she grew, instead of her catching up with us, we were trying to keep up with her. She has this different way of looking at life that completely blows me away. She's always seeking out success in whatever it is that she's doing by not seeing the obstacles that lie before her.

I remember once we were having a dinner theater at our church, which should have had servers, but didn't. And even though she was quite young, I believe she was only eight at the time of the event, she grabbed a tray and began to serve in such a way that spontaneously people began to give her tips. When she enters into things, that most kids her age are afraid to do, it is her norm. The harder it is, the harder she tries. She never gives thought to her age, or her height, she just sees it; whatever it is she goes after it. When the Lord gave me the title for this chapter it was based on a lesson that God taught me, while listening to a story that was being told to me by my other children concerning their little sister. I'm a mother of five, and this child is the youngest. Many of you would think that's why she is so challenged to do more because she wants to fit in with her older siblings. Part of that may be true but in the heart of this child, God has given her a just-jump spirit.

## Just Run

When I say a just-jump spirit, I mean that whatever the challenge is that comes before you, instead of backing away, just run and take that leap of faith. At the end of the day it will bear the results that you are seeking. I, on the other hand was afraid to jump. Throughout my journey I learned how to throw myself off of cliffs. The higher I climbed in the Lord, there have been moments when I was afraid of the place where He had brought me to. I actually wanted to back up and run, but instead I would grab myself by the nape of my neck and throw myself off of the cliff, in spite of my fear I knew that it was God, and He would catch me. That's pretty much how I have lived my life as an adult. The moment the thought of running comes, and when I say running, I mean abandoning the challenge of whatever it is that has been placed before me. The moment my feet hits the ground to run from whatever it is that God is taking me, I yank myself around and throw myself off the cliff.

When we read the word of God it tells us that He equips those He calls, meaning that whatever he places before us we have the ability to accomplish it. Without telling my whole life story, there are some things that I have to share with you concerning my youngest daughter. First, I am happily married to an amazing man who is not seen often because he works out of state and comes home only a couple of times a month. And because of this strange-but God arrangement, we have a home in Texas, and in another state. So in the summer, when our children are out of school they split time here with me in Texas and with my husband out of state.

One summer in particular, when my children went for their regular summer visit, my husband was working in a mountainous area with beautiful rivers and streams. So he would often take our children swimming. All of my children can swim but my youngest daughter was not a very good swimmer at the time so she wore a swimsuit with built in floatation devices which gave us some sense of assurance/security because she was that child that not only wanted to swim in the deep waters, but in entrance to the pool or lake, she wanted to do the flips, stand on chairs and jump into the waters, try to touch the bottom of the deep end, she is that child. When the story was told to me I had the understanding that they were only swimming but as time went on, as the summer progressed, it slipped out that they were cliff diving. Not just the teenagers, but the youngest one as well. As the story unfolds, the older children reached a height where they would go no further; but the youngest persisted to go higher and higher.

## Experience the Jump

As a matter of fact, my husband said at one height it made him nervous, but she wanted to try and he didn't want to stop her. My husband believes that the reason why many adults live such fearful lives and shun away from challenges is because their parents impart fear into them. So because of him not wanting to make her afraid he let her try while securing the safety of the jump. While my husband was treading water in the area where she would land, there was a gentleman higher instructing the jumpers on how to cliff dive at that level. When I talked to my daughter concerning this jump at that height, I'm talking about a jump of 30-60ft from the ground I asked her weren't you afraid?" She told me that she was, and that it made her nervous, but she wanted to experience that jump. And so even though she was afraid she climbed to a height that she had never gone to before with knees knocking and heart pounding. She wanted to experience the jump and she refused to allow fear to stand between her and that experience. Now when she told me the story it made me sick on the inside. I thought of all of the things that could have gone wrong. Her suit wouldn't support her because she was jumping from such a great height or that she would strike a rock and be hurt in a way that could have affected her for the rest of her life. When I started to say to myself if I would have been there she never would have done that, I quickly realized that because of my fears, I would have robbed her of that moment.

I mean how often do you see that happening? And what courage it must take to go beyond what the average individuals were doing to stretch yourself beyond your fears and just jump. She was totally aware that she could have been hurt, but the experience meant more. Now in the eyes of others it may look as if my husband was being irresponsible, but I think that's how life really should be lived. God will bring us to places and position us for things that will cause our knees to knock and our hearts to almost beat out of our chest, and in that moment a decision has to be made.

Will I go with God and experience the eyes have not seen, ears have not heard, wonderful things that he has in store? Or will I back away because I'm just too afraid of the jump? The places that I could easily navigate myself through, and the things that I can do that come at no risk and cost me nothing, are not the places that I could trust God and usually aren't the places that bring great advancement. God is where others aren't standing. He is at heights that are uncomfortable and even unknown to man. It's those places, where we can't see how in the world we could get it done, where we feel so inadequate, so small, where God resides and desires that we reside there with him. It's the places where you realize that one wrong turn, one step off course, could mean the end of everything. But when the Lord says for us to take up our cross and follow Him, it often means journeying down a path where no one will understand but God alone. Where you risk it all for the cause of Christ.

If you think within yourself, how many things have you backed away from because you were too afraid or you couldn't see yourself doing one thing or the other? There was no example or template for you to follow, but God was beckoning or calling you to the unknown.

And because of fear of the unknown you withdrew and turned and went in another direction, and asked God to bless it even though you knew fully that it wasn't quite what God had in store for you. You have even tried to make yourself comfortable where you are, but you found no comfort there. You even resorted to trying to push others down a path that you were afraid to go. When I think of how that sweet little girl just took that jump, it changed something in me. And instead of just throwing myself off of the cliff in many situations, I now willingly walk up with my own knees knocking and heart pounding out of my chest and I take the jump risking it all. It's so funny how once you jump, on the way down; the thoughts are not in your mind of how you're going to save yourself. The thoughts come in reassuring you, that God's got you and everything is going to be alright and when you land in the spot where you were destined for that moment or season in time you become so grateful that you took the leap. One of the things we have to quit doing is over analyzing situations based on our past experiences. Or the experiences of others whom we have watched try in areas where they believe that they have heard from God and fail. Their experiences cannot be used as reasons not to trust God. You don't even know if they really heard from God, or if they followed the full instructions from God. Many times people will say they heard from God but they fail to tell you that they didn't follow all the instructions in which God gave them. It's when they look at their lives in a failed state and verbalize they heard from God. It appears as though God let them down when in actuality we have to follow all of the instructions to see the fulfillment of what God has for us.

## When I Land He is There

If you remember, I shared with you that when my daughter reached a certain level there was someone in place who instructed her on where to step and instructed her on what she needed to do for a successful jump. And God is that one in our lives who instructs us every step of the way so when our feet are standing at the edge of the cliff He is the one that is instructing us on what to do to take the step. But even better than that, we don't go off of the cliff alone, He goes with us. And not only does He go with us, He is there standing in the very spot where we will land. Our God is an omnipresent God, and He will never send us somewhere where He will not be waiting for us when we get there. Remember He is in your past, in your present, and in your future. All at the same time. You will never have to do it alone. He is like a fence, a gate, a wall of protection around you. So when fear comes, to tell you that once you step out in a way that you have never stepped before, that it won't work out, and that God won't be there, shake yourself and say, "He's already there and He's with me now." Refuse to miss out on another moment because you're too afraid to jump. Don't allow the things that have been natural hindrances for others to be your hindrance.

I had an experience in my own life, where I was required to take a leap at a level that I had never taken before. And when I hit the ground, I thought God wasn't there. But the Word of the Lord says, "That all things work together for the good of those who love the Lord and that are called according to His purpose." And even though I felt like in that moment I had missed God Because I didn't keep all of the instructions that He had given me, instead of me arriving at the place where He desired for me, God is so good that he just used it as a learning exercise. Over the years He has been coaching me, preparing me, challenging me to climb back up, and take the jump again. For me this book is a prime example, because I am dyslexic. Therefore reading and writing is sometimes difficult for me. It would be easy for me to say that the odds are against me. And it would be understandable if I became frustrated, and chose not to do this, because it's challenging enough when you're not dyslexic or you're not a person who's all over the place most of the time. But I just jumped, knowing the season and the time was now to jump, trusting that God was with me when I stood at the edge of this cliff and will be standing with me when I touch the ground. I have made a personal vow to myself that whatever God tells me to do in this season I will do. I will break the hands of the enemy off of my arms and legs in the Spirit and I will leap from victory to victory in the Lord.

There will be nothing that God has planned for me that I will not allow myself to experience because of fear and insecurity. When we look back over our lives we can see places where the enemy has robbed us of great experiences that we should have had in the Lord. But you must come to yourself quickly, and say I will not give away another day to fear of failure, nor moments of inadequacy, I will trust God and walk in everything He has planned for me. So where is the precipice that you are standing at the edge of and God is requiring you to take your leap from? What is it that's holding you back?

## What Lie Is It?

The place where fear grips you and the opinions of others arrest you from being all that God wants you to be. What lie is it that you have to fight off daily that keeps you from soaring to heights that you've never gone to before? What lie has the enemy told to you in your childhood that keeps you grounded unable to climb to new heights and take leaps that other men are too afraid to do? Disassemble those lies and move forward. Get a visual picture in your mind of where that place is that God wants you to be and begin to violently rip the chains that have held you bound off of yourself. So that you may enter into every promise God has made you.

Start first by removing the chains from your mind. Change the way you think, when you change the way you think it will change the way you respond. Then tear the chains away from your heart so that you can receive the truth and detach yourself from the lie. Now break the chains off of your feet and hands so that you can move forward with haste in the direction in which God is calling you. Once you have fresh new thoughts and after your heart has been freed, then your physical body will move in the direction in which God is beckoning. In this season of my life I'm probably freer than I've ever been because I see it differently, and my heart has embraced the truth concerning myself and the will of God in my life. I'm ready, and I would like for you to be ready for every challenge that God places before us understanding that God will guarantee success as we follow the roadmap that He has placed before us that will carry us to heights that will bring us to a place of the greatest jump of all. Remember you were created to be Unstoppable.

# Chapter 9

## Ṝ

# The Truth

Truth. What is Truth? The truth is the exact opposite of a lie. Your foundation that your unstoppable life is built upon is truth. So for a moment let's discuss what truth is. The truth that I am sharing with you is based on what the Word of God says about us.

In Psalms 139:14, The Psalmist starts out by saying, "I praise you because I am fearfully and wonderfully made. Your works are wonderful and I know that full well."

The psalmist was saying that he gave God the praise because he was fearfully and wonderfully made. He was declaring that there were no errors involved in his creation. No matter what he had to contend with he knew for himself that He was made in a way that reflected the wholeness of who God was.

## Awesomeness

As we journey down this path to unstoppable, we have to understand the awesomeness of who we are. Even though you've heard it many times before through the voices of teachers and preachers, that God did not create us to be weak, or to see ourselves as less than who we truly are. Many of us see ourselves as inferior, broken and fragmented. We look at the lives of others and measure ourselves by their success, when in fact who they are has nothing to do with who I am. When the psalmist wrote to be fearfully made it means I have a respect or reverence for God. It brings us to a place of thanksgiving, a knowing that God does not randomly place people into this world without regard. In other words, you did not just happen without Him giving thought to you. When you look at your life and you feel as though you are a complete failure, it is in complete conflict with the nature of God. When you don't see yourself as good enough those very thoughts are a complete contradiction with how our God works. DO you honestly think that the God who put so much care in a single blade of grass, that will just fade away, the same God that would put attention and time in creating beautiful flowers and placing them in some of the remote regions in the earth that man will never look upon, would not give you the same care? He has called us to be His witnesses in the earth.

The enemy works overtime trying to convince us that we are unworthy to be used by God, unworthy to fulfill His plan, but we are not. In the scripture it says that I am fearfully and wonderfully made. Wonderful means to be distinct or unique. The psalmist knew that there was no one else like Him. He knew how special he was to God, and how much care went into his creation. If you are going to move into this position of unstoppable you have to see the uniqueness of your design. You have to embrace the care and the attention in which the Master used in creating you. Say to yourself, I am not an afterthought in the mind of God. But when He created me, it was with care and attention. My design. Not like anyone else's. Unique. Throughout our lives, there is this presence that is always in place trying to tear us down, trying to silence the voice of truth that echoes down in the depths of me. I was created in His image and regardless of what is spoken over my life there is more to me than it appears.

## Reinforcement

I remember listening to an interview where Maria Shriver was discussing the relationship she had with her parents, and when she spoke about her father, it reminded me of the relationship that we should have with The Lord. I remember her saying that every time she came into her parents' presence her father would always tell her how wonderful she was, how lucky her friends were to have her as a companion, and how fortunate the man that she was married to was to have her as his wife. Then he would ask her did they know how fortunate they all were for them to be a part of her life. She went on to say that one day she asked her dad as she was leaving, why did he always say and do those things. I'm quite sure she knew that he loved her. This is the part of the interview that I will always remember. Her father's reply was the world is hard enough on us you're always up against negative things that are being said or done. So when she was in his presence, he made sure that she was built up and praised by her family, so that when those times would come, they wouldn't be quite as difficult because of all of the reinforcement she had received in love. God's desire is that we not embrace the opinions and views of others beyond what He has said and what He does for us. But often times we choose the opinions of man rather than standing on the truth of the word of God. If you're having a bad day you're more receptive to negativity that comes your way. Many times it may come from the very ones who are closest to you. Your spouse, family members, or spiritual leaders, but if we are to move forward, our reality must be bound to the truth.

## My Fence

In Romans 8:31, What shall we say of such things as these, if God is for us whoever can be against us?" In that very scripture it is declaring that we are unstoppable. It's saying that if the very God of the universe is on your side, what could possibly get in your way to stop you from accomplishing everything He has created you to do. Let's give this some thought. Who is greater than God? Who has more power than God? A being who is omnipresent and has the ability to be in your past, present and future all at the same time; When you look at Him in that way, it's impossible for those that believe in Him to live defeated lives.

A songwriter wrote a song asking Jesus to be a fence all around him. When you look at the omnipresence of the Lord, that's exactly what God is in our lives. We stand in the center while He wraps himself from my beginning to my end. He's at both ends of my life all at the same time. In Romans, Paul says if God be for us, as if he is giving this thought to the Master of the universe, being your greatest cheerleader or your team member not just someone sitting off to the side, a spectator to your life. I believe the writer sees in his thoughts for that very moment that nothing is impossible with God. I remember the first time that I read that scripture, I felt so empowered. To think that if the Master of the universe were on my side, that I would virtually be unstoppable. The writer wasn't saying "if God" as if to say there's a possibility that He's not. He was actually consumed with the thought of if God is for us, with the understanding that God is for us because we are His children, created by His hands, then nothing or no one can stop us. If God has chosen for me to blessed, who can stop me? If God has laid out a path where He wants my life to end up, who can stand in the road and halt the plans of God? No one.

In Romans 8:33 it says who dare accuses whom God has chosen for His own. It goes on to say no one. For God himself has given us right standing with himself. In reading that I'm not looking from an outward perspective, but from inward. Not even the thoughts that I think about myself, the feelings that I have concerning me don't change the views or opinions that God has concerning me. Have you ever had someone speaking positively into your life and while they were speaking these things concerning you, in between every line and word that was spoken, you would say something completely opposite? For example, they would say how beautiful you are and you would say yeah but, I'm over weight, or my hair's a mess. The word of the Lord says that when He declares a thing it is so. So when He says that I am fearfully and wonderfully made, there should not even be anything that conflicts with this statement.

## God Is Not a Liar

Because any word that conflicts with what God is saying concerning me would imply that God is a liar and every sane individual should know that God is not a liar. Yet, it is still easier for us to believe the negative report concerning us, than it is to receive the truth in which God has spoken over us. And that is where the true battle lies. It's so hard for us, to see the good in us when we are looking at ourselves as natural beings and not seeing ourselves delivered from natural boundaries because we serve a super natural God. When you come up against a situation in which you can't solve the problem, if you can't see yourself in the context of God that problem appears to be unsolvable. But when you see yourself hidden in the context of who God is, then it is easy to see that your wisdom is not limited. Because all of your resources even the answers to every problem comes from the wisdom of God. And when you are His, everything that belongs to God, you have right to. And God's resources are unlimited.

## Life in My Words

I remember having a conversation with Bishop I.V. Hilliard, concerning my state of being in that present moment and as I begin to describe to him what my struggle was, every time I would say I did not have or I was not able to he would always say to me don't say that, don't speak that. To me I was just trying to be descriptive in explaining what was going on, but he was trying to block the very words that were in conflict with the word of God, so every time that I would try to speak in conflict with what God had already said or who I was in Him, this pastor would stop me. At first I didn't quite understand what he was doing and the more I would try to explain the more he would stop me, and I was becoming frustrated. But as time went on it became clear, I was so programmed to speaking how I felt and gauging situations based on what I saw in the natural, that it was forming a reality and was in conflict with what God had spoken and intended for my life. How often do you do this very thing?

In Proverbs 18:20 (NIV) it says the tongue has the power of life and death and those that love it will eat its fruit. Which is to say that, I can form a life with my words that either walks in line with what God has spoken over me, or in conflict with what God has spoken.

And what Bishop Hilliard was saying was for me not to create a situation of defeat where God had already given me victory.

In Romans 23, Paul says:

And we believers also groan, even though we have the Holy Spirit within us as a foretaste of future glory, for we long for our bodies to be released from sin and suffering. We, too, wait with eager hope for the day when God will give us our full rights as his adopted children,[a] including the new bodies he has promised us.

In this passage it references to future victories, which we have not yet obtained, yet everything insides of us groans for it but there is a victory that is to be gained here and now, a greater place of completeness in the Lord.

In Romans 8:37 it declares that we are more than conquerors, unstoppable. I've heard it put this way: a fighter goes through the process of preparing for a fight by training physically and emotionally. And on the day of the fight he enters the ring against his opponent and if he has applied everything in which his training produced, at the end of the fight he would be victorious.

At the end of his fight he will have conquered his opponent. To look at him you can see that he paid a very high price for the victory.

But the one that's more than a conqueror is the one who receives full benefit total, access to all that was won, but never trained one day. Never entered the ring at any point in time, didn't suffer at all, but at the end of the fight the check is handed over to them.

The Word says that's who we are. We've done nothing to earn the blessings or the favor of God. He made all of the sacrifices, paid the price for us to be victorious. So how could we be anything less? We are more than conquerors because our God paid the price for it to be so.

The truth is that we are the head and not the tail. We are above and not beneath.

Just as it states in Isaiah 54:

*In righteousness shalt thou be established: thou shalt be far from oppression; for thou shalt not fear: and from terror; for it shall not come near thee. Behold, they shall surely gather together, but not by me: whosoever shall gather together against thee shall fall for thy sake.*

*Behold, I have created the smith that bloweth the coals in the fire, and that bringeth forth an instrument for his work; and I have created the waster to destroy.*

*No weapon that is formed against thee shall prosper; and every tongue that shall rise against thee in judgment thou shalt condemn. This is the heritage of the servants of the Lord, and their righteousness is of me, saith the Lord.*

These passages are saying that I was created in righteousness. I have been established in God, not established in man. Not established in others' opinions and views of me but of the One who matters and because of that I have nothing to be afraid of. In verse 15 it says to be mindful because the enemy will come, thoughts will come, fears will come and trials will come, but when those negative things come into our lives, it's not coming from God. And if it's not coming from God there's no way we can be defeated by it. Every tool that the enemy uses to destroy us, God gave him the ability to develop it. Therefore God has the ability to stop him. That is why confidently we know that it doesn't matter what comes against us, with God on our side, it cannot prosper. It doesn't matter where the negative report comes from in Christ Jesus we have the ability to condemn that Word. This is our heritage, as those who serve God because our righteousness is in Him. In our righteousness is our authority. It doesn't matter what the enemy tries to throw at us, the truth of God is just the truth.

Today I want to challenge you to dispel every lie that the enemy has told you, every negative thought that you've thought about yourself, and even your thoughts concerning others. It's time for us to be released into unstoppable. For us to soar beyond the lies in which we have worked so hard to make our reality. What's the worst that could happen? That you'll come out better than you were before? If you're going to be held hostage, refuse to be your own jailor. Refuse to be the one that places the handcuffs and shackles on your hands and feet. Don't stand a prisoner in a life where you have the key. It's time to for you to live a life that's unstoppable.

# Chapter 10

## Ṝ

# The Reveal

There comes a time in your life when all of the things that you have gone through finally begin to make sense. It's as if you've been traveling down a stream heading in a direction that you weren't quite sure where you would end up, and then one day you were there.As we journey down paths that we feel are God that sometimes end up just being us, God has a way of using the time that was spent away from His plan and purpose for our life to become useful tools which help us to end up right where He intended from the start. He used every wrong decision, every impatient move that we make trying to find that place that we were longing to be in, but we didn't have the clarity nor understanding of what it really was.

That moment in time that we sought after was actually the unveiling. We were desperately trying to get to the place that made sense.

I remember as a young adult I had multiple jobs because I was always seeking that place. Where is it? What is it? The thing that answered all things in me. I could feel it inside of me straining, to be in that certain place or do this certain thing.

The place where I would feel complete. I couldn't wait for it to come. I think that is just how we were built. God places it on the inside of us and even from the womb we are straining to get there. You see it happen in children, when they are trying to dress up in their parents' clothes, pretending to be teachers, or doctors or lawyers. There is something on the inside of them that they are actually after and really don't know what it is. From that moment until the moment that God reveals that place, we seek after it, we strain towards it, we pray for it. There are those that believe that they have missed that moment, that they will never see it because the opportunities have passed them by.

## Flight Time

I remember one time the Lord spoke to me and said that everyone gets his or her flight time. Some find their way early because God reveals the call early, and then there are those whose eyes and ears aren't opened until later in life. Then God is able to reveal to them who they are and what they are called to be. I remember Him saying to me that it doesn't matter when it comes, that we all get flight time. He was referencing us to birds or eagles, because we will all have our moment to soar. The difference between the one who finds their call early, and the one who finds their call later in life is the amount of flight time. Not whether we get the opportunity to fly it's how long we get to fly. I remember the moment when it all came together for me. I had been pastoring in my very first pastorate position, in my tenth year when it just hit me. No longer was I in a place where I was scrambling and trying to figure things out and trying to please people and trying not to fail. I remember the moment when it hit me and I suddenly knew that I was made for it. Now someone would say that after ten years, surely you would know that you could do the job. But I'm not talking about merely doing a job. Sure you can go to work and be there for 20 years and do an excellent job, but there is something different about when God reveals to you that you were made for, created for, the actual place where you are standing.

## Changing The Game

When that moment hits you it changes the game. When you're in the place where you are created to be, you have the power to change lives. You are no longer like an individual thrust into the middle of the ocean floundering and trying to save their own life but when you know that you were made for it; it goes from you just trying to survive in the middle of the ocean to being a lifesaver to others that are drowning around you. You become the one with the answers when you stand in a place that you were made for. In that moment of unveiling it's as if everything inside of you, every fiber of your being becomes in agreement with that moment. Your vision becomes sharp, you see things that you've never seen before, and your understanding becomes clear. You are able to hear conversations and maneuver things differently than you had before because you go from just trying to survive, to being able to control the moment. Because you were made to operate in power and authority in the place that God has set aside for you. The crazy thing is many times other people recognize us before we recognize ourselves. Others have peeked underneath the cloth that's blanketing our lives keeping us hidden, and they have seen who we are before we even know.

### Wisdom

One day I while I was heading to the church and my mind was on a situation that I was going to have to address. I remember the Lord speaking to me softly and lovingly, telling me that I had wisdom. When He said that it was like I had been driving in a rainstorm with the windshield wipers off. I could barely see the way but when the Lord spoke to me the wipers came on and it became clear. Little did I know that I was no longer merely doing a job but I was on the pathway to my calling. It's frustrating going through life unsure of where you belong. Not knowing who you are and God so desperately desires to reveal it to you. The problem is not that He doesn't want to show you who you are it's just until you are ready, He can't. Because revealing to you who you are, goes hand in hand with Him revealing who He is and how those two have to work together. There are many who want the reward or benefit of the blessing without coming in close contact with the Blesser. And if you don't believe that's true you can tell the difference between a leader who was created for leadership, and a leader who stands in the position merely because man placed him there. There's a difference in the passion for the position. One is there for the betterment of the company or project and the other is there for their own personal reward. Whenever God gifts you that gifting is never about you. And the one that that has been revealed to realizes that. Their gift goes far beyond them. And it reaches into the lives of others.

## Set Place

For most of my young life, I was a professional

dancer and so I had been trained for performance. But when I grew older, I watched another dancer who probably didn't have the technical experience that I had, but she had been gifted by God. And when she danced, it was explosive. It was so explosive and impactful that people's lives were changed just by watching her, and experiencing her in her moment of dance. I had never seen anything like it. It was both powerful and scary to experience. Because it required something of me while she danced. It was if she reached out into the audience and drew you into the performance. Whether you are a dancer by trade, or a spectator that happened to be in the performance it awakened something on the inside of you. There is a difference between being talented and gifted and a difference between being gifted and anointed. In the unveiling of your gift comes a great anointing that allows you to break through natural barriers that have been put in place by man. It permits you to reach into the depths of individuals' lives, destroying strongholds of misinformation concerning themselves, and their placement in life. I'm sure that while sitting in that audience there were people there who were possibly called to be dancers, who gave up because they couldn't see the bigger picture or because obstacles were in their way. But when she danced, it pulled out the dancer in you and you wanted to just stand up in the midst of her performance and join in with her turning it from a performance to a great celebration of what was down in the depths of you.

When you are unveiled it drives not only who you are to the surface, but it drives others and challenges them to want to be their best to be in their set place. When you are unveiled those who were watching you who knew you in times past are then provoked to say where is my place? When is my time? When you began to ask those questions God begins to move on your behalf. When you are no longer content with just getting by, no longer comfortable in that place you are in God will reveal himself wholly and completely for you and begin to move on your behalf.

## Gods' Gifts

I remember on a hospital visit where one of my members was preparing for surgery. As I stood by their bedside, the surgeon entered into the room just to brief them on all that was going to take place during surgery. And before he exited the room he asked if it would be alright if we had prayer. I being the pastor, assumed he meant would I pray. But that wasn't his intention. He reached for our hands and began to cry out to the One who had gifted him with the ability to be a great surgeon. He understood that he was not just representing himself but he had been given a gift to change the lives of people. Not just in a natural way but in a supernatural way. And unashamedly, he cried out for God's assistance and then sealed the deal by saying in Jesus' name. I couldn't even enter completely into the prayer with Him because I was so blown away by his ability to humble himself in front of his patient and her family as if to say I don't have all of the answers but I know who does. And my trust is in Him. When I tell you my mind was blown, it was truly blown. He wasn't crying out of desperation, this man has a great reputation for being a great surgeon. But one day in his journey there was an unveiling of who he really was. He was no longer a young adult going to med school or doing his residency. He had an encounter with the One who made him and it was revealed unto him what he was created for in an instant. An unveiling of a great godly surgeon was placed on the scene.

## God's Plan

It's powerful when our eyes are opened to the awesomeness of God's plan for our lives. We are not aimlessly running around in the earth realm but we are birthed out with purpose and plan from God almighty and covered in the blood of Jesus so that we might be able to accomplish this plan and be victorious.

My life became full at the unveiling of who I was. My vision became clear. The enemy's desire is to have you to settle. Settle in a place that God never intended for you to settle to do no more than what you can do on your own. To cause you to live a life where reaching for the stars is foolishness. But the moment you are shaken free from the place of just merely trying to survive from day to day, to the realization that God has so much more God will reveal to you where He really desires to take you. Before the Lord actually begins to speak to us concerning all that He has in store for us I love the fact that He takes his time to build our confidence in Him. I've learned that it is important that we have great confidence in God. He won't let us fail because that He desires the best for us. When the enemy chime in using others to persuade us in directions that are opposite of where God is trying to take us, not based on the Word of God, but based on their own life experiences we are not persuaded.

## God Knows the Plan

When I am confident and sure, no matter what they say or do can turn me. If I hold on to God, I know that what He has planned for me, I will see. When I read in Jeremiah 29:11, it states: "For I know the plans I have for you, declares the lord, plans to prosper you and not harm you, plans to give you a hope and a future"
When He says that I know the plans I have for you, He's saying even though you can't see it and even though others may not see it He knows the plans. And one day He'll unveil the plans and those plans will be good plans. Those plans will prosper our lives and they won't bring us to destruction. They will bring us to a place of hope and a great future. No matter how frustrated we are now, you're on a path headed towards a great unveiling even as these thoughts come to mind it creates an excitement within me. Even what He has revealed to me

thus far concerning my own life, there is still so much more that He has not shown. And just the mere fact that God still has great things in store that we don't know about that we've not heard about, that we have never even thought about, makes life exciting and worth living. And then to only imagine even after this life here in the earth He still has even greater in store for us in eternity.

I know this statement because in 1 Corinthians 8:9 *Which none of the princes of this world knew: for had they known it, they would not have crucified the Lord of glory. But as it is written, Eye hath not seen, nor ear heard, neither have entered into the heart of man, the things which God hath prepared for them that love him.*

In that passage it is telling us that there is so much more, and that God holds the key. Think about it. When you look at your own life, do you think where you are is all that God has for you? Even if you are at the pinnacle of your career, there is still so much more. I remember having a vision one time of the completion of a project that God had shown me that He had given me the ability to be able to do and I was so excited. Because the vision stood as a confirmation that I would see it to it's end. In the vision my oldest was standing on the sidewalk and it was clear to me that I was no longer alive. People were greeting him because it was a memorial service for me in a building that we built. I remember having this feeling of completion in the midst of the vision knowing that I had completed it before I died. I began to thanking the Lord, for showing me what was to come and as I was doing that I remember hearing Him speak to me and say if that's all you want me to do, that's fine. But My desire is to do so much more. He was basically saying that I was so fixated on completing the one task and seeking reassurance that we would actually get it done, that I had failed to look beyond that place as if it was all He had for me.

As I grow older, it seems as if the clock moves a lot faster. So within myself I sometimes wonder will I really have time to do all that God has placed in my heart. But then I come to myself and I realize that He did not unveil my destiny for me to see it in part but He revealed it so that I could see it to the end. Remember age is not an issue when it comes to God. God will put people in place to hold up your arms in your moments of weakness, so that He can complete the work that He has begun in you. So now it is time to begin your journey toward an unstoppable life, knowing God is unstoppable is motivation enough. Live your unstoppable life.

# Unstoppable

# Quotes

# &

# Notes

1. "Not every report comes from God, so be sure to stand on the word that comes from Him." Isaiah 40:8

_____

_____

_____

_____

_____

_____

2. "The wounds of our past hold us like chains binding a prisoner from escaping but the blood of Jesus brings release."
(John 8:36)

_____

_____

_____

_____

_____

_____

3. "I will not be a hostage to anything when Jesus has made me free to everything."
(Galatians 5:1)

_____

_____

_____

_____

_____

_____

4. "Empowered to do greater, your season your time."
(1 John 4:4)

_____

_____

_____

_____

_____

5. "Do you know what "oh so close" looks and feels like? That moment right before the breakthrough? Well it looks just like this, the very place where you are standing right now that's why we can't afford to walk away or give up because we have no idea of the very next moment is it."(Galatians 6:9)

---

---

---

---

---

6. You don't need anyone to cosign on your dreams, Jesus has already paid the bill. (Psalms 1:1-3)

_____

_____

_____

_____

_____

_____

7. Your enemy doesn't stop just because God has given you what's been promised. He's fighting you now to take it back. Remain steadfast. (Isaiah 54:17)

_____

_____

_____

_____

_____

_____

8. Has the devil ever tried to put you in a box and use the people you love to sit on the lid? If you've ever had to fight at least one battle and come out on top, lift your hands in the air and say, "I'm not going in, I'm going to win!" (2 Chronicles 20:15)

_____

_____

_____

_____

_____

_____

9. Don't let the woes of yesterday's struggles; rob you of the promises today. Call those things that be not as though they were and live victoriously in Christ. (Romans 4:7)

_____

_____

_____

_____

_____

_____

10. Be grateful for where you are now, but don't settle for your best, strive for God's best. (3 John 1:2)

_____

_____

_____

_____

_____

_____

11. Fear of failure and poor self image will tell you where you are is good enough. While God's extravagant love sits on the shelf waiting for you. (Deuteronomy 20:3-5)

_____

_____

_____

_____

_____

_____

12. We serve an extravagant God who blesses extravagantly. Keep that in mind when Satan tries to make you settle.
(Jeremiah 29:11-12)

_____

_____

_____

_____

_____

13. God handpicked you for this trial and equipped you to win. Therefore your victory is guaranteed. How awesome is that?
(1 Peter 2:9)

_____

_____

_____

_____

_____

_____

14."One step backwards is one too many.  (Isaiah 43:18-19)

_____

_____

_____

_____

_____

**UNSTOPPABLE**

15. Before someone is able to see your worth and value you, you must first be able to see your own worth and value yourself.
(Psalms 139: 13-16)

_____

_____

_____

_____

_____

_____

16. Many people wait on others to validate them when God already has.
(2 Corinthians 12:9)

_____

_____

_____

_____

_____

_____

17. Celebrate the work that your Father has done by celebrating yourself.
(Psalms 139:14)

_____

_____

_____

_____

_____

_____

18. If being your self is not good enough for others the problem is not yours, it's theirs. God knew just what He was doing when He created you. Rejoice in your individuality, God has. He's the one that made you, and all of His works are masterpieces.
(Psalms 139:13)

_____

_____

_____

_____

_____

19. "It's pointless to walk around under the pressures of live when you have the authority to move every mountain that stands in your way."(Matthew 21:21)

_____

_____

_____

_____

_____

_____

20. Don't give up on believing on what God promised. Man breaks promises but God never will. (Numbers 23:19)

_____

_____

_____

_____

_____

_____

21. Don't judge us too harshly based on what you see. At first glance David probably didn't look like a king. But he was called to royalty. Just because we don't look like much now, doesn't mean this is where we will remain. (Matthew 7:1-3)

_____

_____

_____

_____

_____

_____

22. God's child in a ditch is more valuable than the world's child on a mountaintop, if God be for you who can be against you.
(Romans 8:31)

_____

_____

_____

_____

_____

23. The enemy wages war against us daily. So when he shows up, don't be taken back by his actions. Hit the door swinging before he even has a chance to knock. We are more than conquerors.
(Romans 8:37)

_____

_____

_____

_____

_____

_____

24. Sometimes the ones who should love you best do the worst job at it. Place yourself in the hands of the One who loves you most: the Lover of your soul.  (John 3:16)

_____

_____

_____

_____

_____

25. It's not necessary for man to know of your wounds, especially since there's nothing he can do about it. Let God be your healer. (Isaiah 53:5)

_____

_____

_____

_____

_____

_____

26. Don't disqualify yourself because you don't look the part. God's sees what's inside of you.  Time to get in the game.
(1 Samuel 16:7)

_____

_____

_____

_____

_____

_____

27. Looking to the left or the right isn't a definitive indicator of where you are. Focus on the finish and keep pushing.
(1 Corinthians 9:26)

_____

_____

_____

_____

_____

_____

28. Remember that your trials are necessary to equip you for the battles ahead. Embrace them knowing that they are reinforcing your ability to endure. (James 1:2)

_____

_____

_____

_____

_____

_____

29. God is waiting for you to empty yourself of burdens and broken places, so He can fill you up with joy and wholeness.
(Isaiah 61:3)

_____

_____

_____

_____

_____

_____

30. It's time for you to acknowledge what God has placed inside of you, and begin operating at your unstoppable level. He's given you what it takes, let the deposit manifest. (Deuteronomy 20:4)

_____

_____

_____

_____

_____

# Acknowledgements

**I would like to acknowledge the editing team that made this possible. For the countless hours that you all put in to ensure that this book happened. So, Yulanda Davis, Tiffany Reyna & Cheritha Reed, I want to say Thank You!**

# Special Thanks

**To Anthresia (Sugar), this book would still be words in my heart without you. For your time, patience and commitment, thank you!**

**I would thank the photographer Frank Harrison and Joshua Lemmons for the graphics**

# About The Author

Regina Johnson is the founding pastor of The Father's House with a rapidly growing membership currently in two locations. Her ministry is expanding rapidly throughout Southeast Texas. She has been in ministry as a Sr. pastor for over fourteen years. Mrs. Johnson has an exceptional heart for the people of God and her vision is to impact and change a nation.

Mrs. Johnson has overseen several ministries and pastors on her journey and is currently preparing pastors for future church plants. This also includes a young pastor in India who is giving her an avenue to spread the gospel abroad.

Regina Johnson is currently working on her Doctorate of Theology. She has been married to Joe Johnson for over 20 years and they have five wonderful children.

www.ingramcontent.com/pod-product-compliance
Lightning Source LLC
Chambersburg PA
CBHW021236090426
42740CB00006B/564